london RESTAURANTS AND THEIR RECIPES

London is as tantalising as ever, especially when it comes to its wealth of culinary delights. Its diverse cuisine offers more than enough opportunities for unforgettable wining and dining. This guide presents a selection of London's best restaurants, from The Atlantic Bar and Grill to Zilli Fish, The Sugar Club to Club Gascon. On top of this, all the restaurants in this book share their chef's favourite recipes, so you can experience the best of London's menus from the comfort of your own kitchen.

We wish to thank everyone, who has in some way or other been involved in creating this book. Of course the chefs who, even though sometimes reluctantly gave their best recipes. Especially we want to thank Christer Elfving for cooking the dish on the cover.

MAAIKE, HARRY & PATRICK

contents

●おいしいお召し上がり方
白鶴サケパックは低温容器ですから、冷蔵庫などに入れ、常温
（5℃くらい）上層（50℃くらい）ぬるかん（40℃くらい）な冷酒
みで冷やして、またいろいろな温度に冷やすことによってうすく
楽しみください。

ハクツル
サケパック
500ml 清酒
アルコール分 15度以上16度未満
日本酒度 キーパー 糖添加アミノー

製造年月は上部に記載

白鶴酒造株式会社H
神戸市東灘区住吉南町四丁目五番大野

restaurant index

starters

chilled **AUBERGINE SOUP** with yoghurt and paprika **69**

puree of **AUBERGINE** **105**

BOBOTIE SALAD **111**

CALAMARI chilli fry with coconut **59**

CASHEW NUT PAKODAS **103**

bang bang **CHICKEN** **95**

steamed **DIM SUM RIBS** **107**

EGG and **CHUTNEY PATTIES** **121**

thai **FISH CAKES** **49**

FLAT BREAD **123**

smoked **HADDOCK** and welsh rarebit **71**

tartare of **MACKEREL** with **SMOKED SALMON**, crème fraîche and caviar **57**

MUSSELS, cucumber and dill **113**

PASTA 'STRACCI' with pesto sauce **65**

stuffed **PIQUILLOS PEPPERS** with brandade and jabugo ham **109**

PIROZHKI **93**

POTATO PANCAKE, smoked salmon, crème fraîche and caviar **79**

mini **SALMON** and **SMOKED HADDOCK** fish cakes **125**

pea, pancetta, broad bean and goat's cheese **SALAD** **75**

seared **SCALLOPS** with a lemongrass and coconut cream sauce **99**

skewers of **SCALLOPS** with rosemary sprigs **127**

grilled **SEA SCALLOPS** with crispy calamari, sauce nero **97**

thai **SEAFOOD COCKTAIL** **43**

SHIITAKE MUSHROOM BROTH with soba noodles, tofu and prawns **115**

potted **SHRIMP** **67**

chilli salt **SQUID** **61**

peppered **TUNA CARPACCIO** **117**

main courses

layered **AUBERGINES** and **SEA-SCALLOPS** with marina sauce **53**

ripe **BANANA PACHADI** **103**

BIFE ANA, portuguese rumpsteak sandwich **69**

roast **BONE MARROW** with parsley salad **113**

grilled **CALF'S LIVER**, sage and onion mash, sauce diable **109**

roast **CHICKEN** with yoghurt **105**

roast **COD** with olive oil mash **57**

roast **COD** wrapped in smoked paprika pancetta with spinach and cumin lentils **51**

CORNED BEEF hash **95**

stuffed **COURGETTES, AUBERGINES** and vine leaves **85**

stuffed **COURGETTE FLOWERS** **125**

FISH PIE **71**

HAKE KOYKERA **87**

baked **HAKE** with charlotte potatoes, spinach and crab bisque **73**

IHEM LAHLOU (sweet lamb stew) **91**

braised knuckle of **LAMB** with rosemary and garlic cassoulet **81**

braised shoulder of **LAMB** **117**

MASALA PORK **59**

roast **MONKFISH**, stewed beans and lavender **63**

pan-fried skewers of **MONKFISH** **65**

ORECCHIETTE with roasted sweet cherry vine tomato and chorizo **41**

pork and **PINEAPPLE** stir-fry **45**

thai **PRAWN CURRY** **47**

PRAWNS with spring onions **121**

stir-fry **PRAWNS** with lemongrass **107**

RED MULLET stuffed with fennel and citrus zest, tomato and olive sauce **77**

warm **SALAD** of pigeon, chicken livers, chorizo, new potatoes, poached eggs and sherry vinegar **39**

SALMON SASHIMI on spring onion blinis with wasabi crème fraîche and caviar **99**

SALMON soufflé **49**

pan roasted **SALMON**, parsley salad and aioli **83**

grilled **SALMON** with ventreche ham, savoy cabbage, sauce lie de vin **97**

pan fried **SCALLOPS** with beetroot and walnut oil **101**

seared **SCALLOPS**, risotto nero and anchovy spinach **79**

whole **SEA BASS** in salt and pepper crust **127**

SEA BASS with gremolata, puy lentils, spinach and crème fraîche **123**

SHASHLYK PO-KARSKI **93**

SMOKED CHEESE and **ROCKET POLENTA** with roasted root vegetables, garlic and red wine sauce **89**

SPAGHETTI VONGOLE **75**

pan fried **SPRINGBOK FILLET** with butternut, red pepper and leeks **111**

roasted **SWEET BUTTERNUT** squash risotto with new season violetta garlic and coriander **41**

T-BONE MESON BILBAO **87**

seared **TUNA**, courgette fritters and aioli **67**

braised **TURBOT** with champagne and herb noodles **55**

roast breast of **WOOD PIGEON** with truffled jerusalem artichoke puree and madeira sauce **119**

desserts

BLOOD ORANGE and **PASSION FRUIT JELLY** 119

CAPPUCCINO ice cream 39

CHOCOLATE and **HAZELNUT BRÛLÉE** 43

italian **CHOCOLATE** and **AMARETTO PUDDING** with bitter chocolate sauce 53

bitter **CHOCOLATE** and **PICKLED GINGER MOUSSE** 45

dark **CHOCOLATE CAKE** 51

COUSCOUS SEFFA 91

warm croustillant of **FIGS** with pinot noir sauce 101

FRESH FRUIT in star anise syrup 77

sweet **FOIE GRAS** with apple candy 63

LEMON TART 83

MOHALLABIYEH 85

NANAIMO BARS 47

PINEAPPLE CHEESECAKE 81

lemongrass roast **PLUMS** with mascarpone and lime 115

STRAWBERRY jelly with iced yoghurt 55

sweet ginger **TIRAMISU** 61

oking at home • cooking at home • cooking at

ome • cooking at home • cooking at home • c

Who would have thought that we get head chefs to give us their secrets? This remains the dream of every amateur cook. In London we got what we did just that. We covered their restaurants and they gave us their recipes. This book is for everybody who likes good food as well as cooking it. All recipes are for four, unless otherwise stated. At the back of the book you will find a glossary of cooking terms. In this chapter you will find some interesting facts, tips and basic recipes.

what do you need?

Usually those who love cooking have a fondness for kitchen tools as well. In any well-stocked kitchen store you will find beautiful pans, professional cutting boards and much, much more. Amongst the most essential utensils you'll need are sharp knives and a high quality cutting board, made from hardened plastic, marble or glass. You can use a wooden cutting board to cut bread or vegetables, but never use it to for fish or meat. Juices will get into the wood, thus leaving you with a flavoured cutting board! The real pros use cutting boards that are colour coded according to the hardness of the plastic used.

Pans are of equal importance. Never use pans that have a stained bottom, as this is unhealthy. Pans made from cast iron or ones that have a non-stick coating are good for frying. For fish you can use a round pan, as long as your chosen fish fits it. For big fish that otherwise would have their head and tail sticking out you can opt for an oval shaped pan. Pots come in many shapes, a large one for soup or cooking mussels will always come in handy. A wok is ideally suited for making a stir-fry. This method of cooking has gained a firm hold in the English kitchen; greens will stay crunchy, cooking times are very short and you won't have to use much fat!

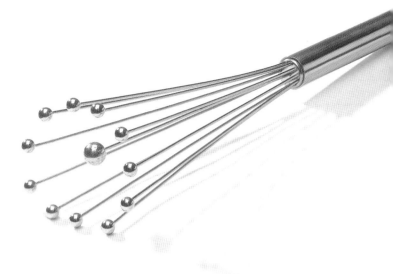

As said; knives should be sharp. There is nothing worse than having to cut with a blunt edge. Small peeling knives can be used for almost everything, a knife with a serrated edge comes in handy for soft products like tomatoes. The use of a bread knife enables you to cut fresh bread without denting it. A chef's knife is good for fish and meat. If it is sharp it will be easy to cut fish and meat into thin slices. A steel or knife sharpener is handy for keeping an edge, but the real honing should be left to the professionals. Many kitchen suppliers will sharpen your knives. Badly sharpened knives won't last you long.

You should also have a couple of spatulas and wooden spoons. Use round ones for stirring, and flattened ones for frying. Beaters or whiskers are needed for making sauces. Choose one that has more wires, it will be more expensive but will whisk smoother. A garlic press will always come in useful, but you can also chop the garlic with a chef's knife. You want to be done quickly? Use a large food processor or a hand-blender with one of those little chopping bowls. Remember that more expensive items are not always better. Those who like Asian dishes should pay a visit to their Asian shop. They quite often stock great kitchen tools, at surprisingly low prices.

oven temperatures

The right oven temperature is very important, so we recommend that you use an oven thermometer. With some dishes that need to be heated or baked no exact temperature is given. Here you'll find a list of the appropriate temperatures.

	MARK	DEGREES CENTIGRADE
LOW HEAT	1	100 - 140
MEDIUM HEAT	2	140 - 180
WARM TO HOT	3	180 - 210
HOT TO VERY HOT	4	210 - 250

weights & measurements

Most European recipes will give measurements in grams and millilitres. Although a good eye and steady hand come in useful when cooking it is advisable to keep to the given quantities. It's especially important to measure precisely when making cakes and pastries. A kitchen scale, postal scale or measuring spoon for small amounts comes in handy as well as a measuring cup with clear markings. Below you will find the most commonly used weights and measurements.

1 KILOGRAM	1.000 grams
1 POUND	500 grams
1 LITRE	1.000 millilitre
1 DECILITRE	100 millilitres
1 CENTILITRE (CC)	10 millilitres
1 WINEGLASS	125 millilitres
1 TABLESPOON	20 millilitres
1 DESSERTSPOON	15 millilitres
1 TEASPOON	10 millilitres

herbs & spices

A simple dish can be turned into something special by adding the right herbs and spices. They should add to the dish and not overwhelm. If you use leaves of fresh herbs its better not to cook them but just stew them for a short time. Stems and roots can be cooked with your soup, or you can stew or sweat them. By experimenting with the herbs listed below you can give a dish a different taste each time you prepare it.

Store dried herbs in a closed container, otherwise they'll lose their smell and taste quickly. You've got a garden or balcony? Grow your own herbs. You can do this in your kitchen also. Once your herbs start to take root, and only basil is tricky, you'll never have to buy dried herbs again. As well as fresh, large supermarkets also stock freezed or freeze-dried herbs, which form a good substitute.

At your Asian shop you'll find a wide variety of herbs that are used in Asian cooking. Basic ingredients are ginger, lemon grass, lemon grass leaves, coriander and Thai basil. You'll find a glossary of the most widely used herbs in this chapter. Asian cooking also uses substitutes for meat like tofu and tempé, which are both made of soybeans. Coconut and coconut milk (either fresh from the nut or simply canned) are good for adding taste as is soy sauce. Ketjap Manis is sweet and can be used for vegetables and meat, while Japanese Kikkoman soy sauce has a more bitter taste and is good with sushi.

Moroccan cooking uses coriander, cinnamon, cumin, mint, star aniseeds and harissa. Arabic cooking is quite spicy but their cakes and desserts tend to be really, really sweet: 'le repos de la gorge'; give your throat a rest. Greek cooking has three main flavours; olive oil, wine and honey with thyme. The latter one is relatively cheap and readily available in England, but only used pure in Greece, rendering it a specialty.

BASIL

aromatic, with a slight taste of cloves. Goes with almost anything but is very good with tomatoes, pasta sauces and tomato soup.

BAY LEAVES

fiery in taste you can use them in stews, marinades and soups. The leaves themselves shouldn't be eaten.

CELERY

is strong and fresh in taste and goes well in soups, egg dishes and salads.

CHERVIL

sweet and herbal with a whiff of aniseed, to be used in soups and salads.

CHIVES

a soft onion-like taste, good for salads and soups but only add after cooking. Also wonderful with sour cream over baked potatoes.

CINNAMON

has an herbal, fiery flavour with a sweet after-taste. Particularly good in desserts and cakes but can also be used for lamb and pork.

CLOVES

are pungent and sweet at the same time. Use for soups in small quantities. A very distinct taste.

CORIANDER

is sweet, oriental and very aromatic in taste. It has gained popularity in the last few years. It combines well with vegetables and soups. The dried form is used extensively in Asian dishes.

CUMIN

has a strong taste and is used in oriental, Moroccan and Greek dishes. Buy either seeds or ground but don't use too much.

CURRY

hot and sharp with a pungent taste this is a blend of spices. Available from mild to very hot. Is great with rice, soup, vegetables or meat.

DILL

fresh with a distinct herbal taste, good for salads and fish (like poached salmon).

DRAGON

bittersweet, delicate herbal taste for soups, salads but also fish and poultry. Used widely in French cooking.

FENNEL

sweet with a taste of aniseed. Goes well in salads, vegetables or with fish.

GINGER

sweet, slightly bitter and very aromatic it is used extensively in Chinese and Thai cooking. It can be bought fresh or powdered.

HARISSA

also known as pimento or pili-pili is a mixture of red peppers, garlic, salt and various herbs. It is used a lot in Moroccan cooking and can be bought at Asian shops.

LAOS

also known as galangal it can be used fresh or dried and is a main ingredient of many curries.

LEMON GRASS

fresh, bittersweet with a strong taste of lemon. Used in salads, sauces and fish or rice dishes.

MARJORAM

strong, herbal and slightly sweet in taste it can be used is soups, sauces and meat dishes.

MINT

soft and fresh with a bit of menthol, it is used a lot as garnish for desserts but can also be incorporated into salads.

NUTMEG

nutmeg tastes like cinnamon and pepper combined, with a strong smell. To be used with meat, cooked vegetables and sauces.

OREGANO

sweeter and more pungent than marjoram it is used extensively in Italian dishes.

PARSLEY

slightly sweet and fresh in taste it can be used for soups, cold and warm sauces and salads. Flat leaf parsley has gained popularity and is stronger in taste. It is used extensively in Moroccan dishes.

PEPPER

fiery hot in taste it can be used for any dish, preferably freshly ground.

ROSEMARY

pungent, sweet with a nice aroma is used mainly in southern dishes and meats.

SAFFRON

herbal and bitter in taste it adds color to fish and rice dishes.

SAGE

has a distinct fresh taste. Used mainly on its own in French and Italian dishes with white meat like calf or chicken.

SESAME

sweet in taste the seeds can be roasted. Good for chicken, fish, salads and bread and cookies.

STAR ANIS

is sweet, fresh and can be used in a variety of dishes like fish, bouillon and southern cooking.

TARRAGON

a strong aniseed taste, good with fish.

THYME

aromatic and bittersweet it can be used in many dishes and goes well with rosemary.

VANILLA

is sweet, herbal in taste and used extensively in sweets.

oil & vinegar

The different varieties of oil you can buy nowadays seem to get larger and larger. Some people to say 'I use only olive oil', whilst others claim that other kinds can be used just as well. There are no set rules. Frying in olive oil is less fattening than using butter, but for deep-frying you don't have to use this more expensive oil.

'Extra vièrge' or 'extra virgin' olive oil is the best choice but the most expensive oil at the same time. You will notice the difference in taste best when used cold, but also when frying you'll taste that extra penny. The 'extra virgin' oil is purer and has been pressed cold. Other varieties have been pressed warm, giving more oil per kilo but of a lesser quality. You should store oil in a dark, cool place with as little air as possible inside the bottle.

New trends have given us other kinds of oil that have been flavoured by the addition of herbs or spices. Orange oil is good for salads whilst nut oil is delicious in dressings. You can also buy sesame seed oil, to be used for oriental dishes, but you should only use small amounts as this oil has a very strong taste.

There are also many kinds of aromatic vinegars, based on herbs used. Add your favourite herbs to any kind of vinegar then leave, until it has soaked up the taste. A quite different form of vinegar is the balsamic vinegar that comes from the town of Modena in Italy. This is something very special and quite expense. You can use it in a variety of ways but a wonderful tip is to use it in a tomato salad, or the classic combination of tomato, mozzarella and fresh basil, with plenty of fresh black pepper.

Normal white vinegar is usually quite harsh to the palate, so you're better off using a wine- or sherry based vinegar. Don't forget the rule for vinaigrette; three parts oil to one part vinegar. What makes a classic vinaigrette is open to debate, but we think it should contain a little mustard and a bit of honey. You can decide what you like most.

Mustard comes in a variety of ways, from mild to very sharp. Some mustards, like the classic French Dijon have the husks still in them. You can also find smoother kinds, like the pungent English Colman's mustard.

So what is olive oil made of? Olives of course! But there are many more things you can do with olives. They originally stem from Greece where they were regarded as being 'pure'. Used as a form of soap in the old days, now we'd much rather eat them filled with peppers or garlic, along with a nice glass of wine. Green olives are not completely ripe and more chewy, as opposed to the fully ripened black ones. Both kinds are eminently edible. You can buy black or green olives at any deli or supermarket, and they're not expensive. One of the best recipes for olives is the classic tapenade. Use it on bread, grilled meat or fish.

Tapenade

250 G BLACK OLIVES • 30 G CAPERS • 6 FILES OF ANCHOVIES • 3 CLOVES GARLIC • 500 ML OLIVE OIL

Blend everything but the olive oil in a blender until smooth. Stir in the olive oil to form a thick mass. This keeps for about 8 weeks in the fridge if you put a layer of olive oil on top. It's best to make up a big batch.

lettuce & salads

In summer or winter, a nice salad forms part of any meal. It is not for nothing that most supermarkets stock a wide variety of mixed lettuce. Wash lettuce only at the last moment and make sure that the leaves are as dry as possible before adding the dressing. It is not a good idea to dress the salad long before the meal. The lettuce may soak up the dressing (a much used excuse) and the lettuce will lose its bite. You're better of serving the (French) dressing aside in a bowl. There are now many varieties of lettuce easily available. Here are some of the more popular ones.

OAK LEAF LETTUCE

nice soft, dark brown leaves that resembles oak leaves. Has a slight taste of nuts and should be mixed with other lettuces for its taste. Can also be used to garnish dishes as it looks great. Don't stew, just eat raw.

CURLY LETTUCE

looks a lot like endive and can be eaten raw or stewed. Has a slightly bitter taste.

ICEBERG LETTUCE

received its name from its crunchy structure. Although it contains quite a lot of water it is still very tasteful. Can be used with a French dressing or try it grilled with some Gruyere cheese!

LOLLO ROSSO, LOLLO VERDE

one is red, the other one green, and both are curly lettuce. Because of their shape they are great for garnishing, but keep in mind that they can be slightly bitter. Only use raw.

ROMAN LETTUCE

the name makes you think of Ceasar Salads, for which it indeed is used. The bigger leaves can be stewed. You'll find this lettuce mainly in southern countries. When stewed the taste will be less pronounced than when eaten raw.

RUCOLA

rucola also comes under the name roquette or rocket. It has small, spiked leaves and a distinct nutty flavour. You'll find it often as part of a mixed salad or stewed, but can be eaten with a subtle French dressing as well.

LAMB'S LETTUCE

this lettuce you will find loose or pre-packaged. It hardly weights anything, tastes very fresh and looks wonderful on your plate. It forms a nice combination with other lettuces but handle it carefully as it breaks easily, which will make it look unappealing. Is also very good combined with chicory.

potatoes

Whilst the French view the potato as a 'real' vegetable, in England they are seen as a more basic ingredient. But the potato, which has only in the last two centuries been accepted as not being poisonous, has a great variety of uses. Cook, bake, steam, deep-fry or mash them; the possibilities are just endless.

Potatoes are usually divided into the categories; floury or firm and anything in between. The soil in which they are grown is important. Potatoes from clay are usually more floury and tasteful than ones grown in sand. For boiling choose a floury potato, and for frying a firm one is more suitable. For French fries use a large, firm potato. Potatoes can also be divided according to sweetness, and often a sweeter potato like the Nicola has more taste than a dryer, flourier potato.

New potatoes are simply potatoes that have been harvested early. They are harvested in early summer. Other kinds are available throughout the year. New potatoes can be eaten with the skin still on, but potatoes that are harvested later in the year should always be peeled. You can keep new potatoes for about two weeks whilst others can be stored for anything up to 6 weeks. Usually new potatoes are labelled accordingly, but if not you can recognize them by their long, oval shape and yellow skin and flesh.

Mashed potatoes are open to debate. You will find that one chef uses more butter than the other, or might add cream or olive oil. All agree that the best variety is the Ratte. Butter should be added warm and you shouldn't mash with a masher but rather use a squeezer. If you use a masher you will damage the structure of the potato. You can also add some warm stock, herbs and tomato paste.

ACCENT

firm potato that is suitable for French fries and gratin, available throughout the year.

BELLE DE FONTENAY

a famous potato with yellow skin and flesh, quite firm but won't keep long.

BINTJE

is another famous potato, available from September through to July, it can be used for everything

BILDSTAR

a potato with a red glow to the skin, floury and available from September through to July.

NICOLA

is very popular and somewhat floury but still quite 'all-purpose'.

RATTE

is French and oval-shaped, quite firm and the potato of choice for mash.

ROSEVAL

a delicacy with its red skin and yellow flesh it is quite firm.

MARIS PIPER

an all purpose potato, firm with a light coloured skin.

KING EDWARD

considered by many to be the king of potatoes. Ideal for roasting, mash, chips or baking and has a strong flavour.

SWEET POTATO

is more a root vegetable from southern America that is used more often nowadays and can be cooked like any potato. The skin can be red, purple or grey. Check that its still firm and smells fresh when buying.

BINTJE

RATTE

BELLE DE FONTENAY

NICOLA

ROSEVAL

33

rice

The time that we ate only white rice (which contains more calories than brown rice), are long and gone. Nowadays you can buy a wide variety of rice that each have their own individual taste, at your local supermarket. Roughly there are three different varieties; long grained rice will be dry and loose after cooking, medium grained rice will be somewhat softer and more moist, whilst round grain rice will be sticky. White rice is eaten usually as an accompaniment to Oriental dishes but you will find that Asia produces a wide array of rice's. Worldwide their are about 120.000 varieties. Here are just a few.

ARBORIO

is the only real rice for risotto. It is a round-grain variety that soaks up a tremendous amount of water. You can buy it at any Italian shop, isn't expensive and essential for risotto.

BASMATI

is a long-grain variety from India that soaks up a lot of water and smells wonderful; the name Basmati means 'Queen of fragrance'.

COUSCOUS

couscous is a form of 'rice' that is used extensively in Moroccan cooking. The real name is 'semoule de blée dur' indicating that it really is a wheat product. A courser version is called 'bolghour' that is used for 'taboulé', a salad with 'bolghour'.

JAPANESE RICE

is also known as sushi rice as it is the only rice you can use to make sushi. It looks like ordinary round-grain rice, which it isn't. The latter variety is used in Spain for paella.

PANDAN RICE

is a long-grain variety from Thailand. It has a distinct fragrance and is used in Oriental dishes.

WILD RICE

is not really a form of rice but a dark brown grain stemming from swamp grass. It has a distinct nutty taste and is mixed often with rice as it is very expensive.

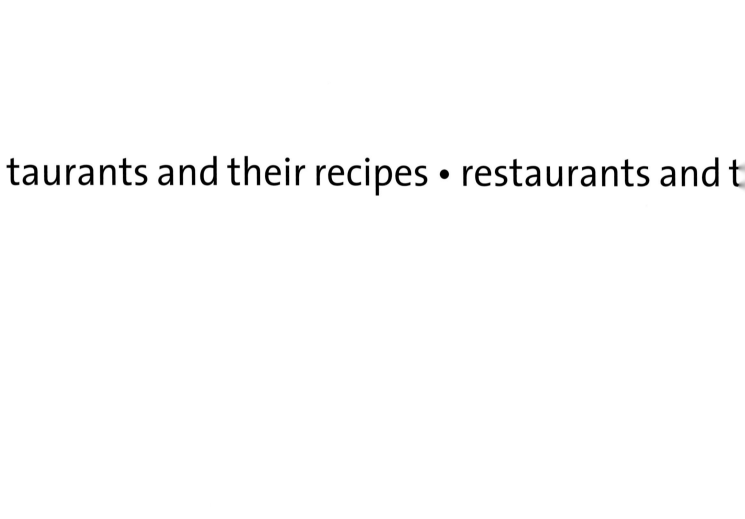
taurants and their recipes • restaurants and t

eir recipes • restaurants and their recipes • res

anglesea arms

OPENING HOURS
MON–SAT 12.30-14.45 & 19.30-22.45,
SUN 13.00-15.45 & 19.30-22.45

CREDIT CARDS
VISA, MASTERCARD

Another exponent of the 'Gastro' pub phenomenon. The Anglesea Arms has consistently managed to stay a few notches above many of its contemporaries. The frill free restaurant to the rear of the pub can only squeeze in around ten tables, so usually during lunch and dinner times, diners spill out and occupy the whole place. This is no surprise when you look at the menus devised and delivered by owner/head chef Dan Evans. Dishes range from simple classics like fish and chips, to the more elaborate such as pigeon terrine with brioche and onion marmalade. But no matter what you opt for, you will enjoy food of the highest quality and cooking. A long, long way from a flat cheese sarnie, and a packet of pork scratchings.

warm salad of pigeon, chicken livers, chorizo, new potatoes, poached eggs and sherry vinegar

Pre-heat the oven to 180°C. Use a thick metal frying pan that can go into the oven. Remove the crust from the bread and tear it into 2.5 cm chunks, toss in a little olive oil and bake for 10-15 minutes. Sauté the pigeon meat (ideally breasts only) in a little vegetable oil until browned, but still pink inside. Put aside to rest. Cut the skinned chorizo into 1 cm dices and sauté in a little olive oil along with the par-boiled, halved potatoes on a medium heat for around 2-3 minutes. Transfer the pan to the oven for around 7-10 minutes, so the paprika in the chorizos turns the potatoes red. Remove from the oven, drain and set aside. Add the chicken livers to the remaining oil and fry until brown on the outside and pink on the inside. Arrange the cooked ingredients on plates with the bitter leaves. De-glaze the pan with the sherry vinegar and pour over the salads. Top with a poached egg and a few croutons.

WINE SUGGESTION DOMAIN AGREE '96, ANJOU VILLAGES

cappuccino ice cream

Beat the eggs, yolks, sugar and Nescafe together. Heat the cream until boiling, then tip onto the egg mixture, beating constantly. Place in a bain-marie and stir for 6-8 minutes until the mix has slightly thickened. Allow to cool by standing in a sink of cold water. Stir occasionally to prevent a skin forming. When it has reached room temperature put into a food processor along with the freshly made, chilled coffee and yoghurt and blend. Churn the mix in an ice-cream machine, and when half frozen add the chocolate (broken into small chunks). Finish and keep chilled before serving.

WINE SUGGESTION BANYULS RIMAGE, LES CLOS DE PANLILLES '96, FRANCE

MAIN COURSE
- HALF A 'RUSTIC' TEXTURED COB
- 2 BONED WOOD PIGEONS OR 4 PIGEON BREASTS
- 2 LARGE LEON CHORIZOS
- 24 NEW POTATOES
- 15 FRESH TRIMMED CHICKEN LIVERS
- MIXED SEASONAL BITTER SALAD LEAVES
- 1 TABLESPOON JEREZ SHERRY VINEGAR
- 4 MEDIUM FREE-RANGE EGGS
- OLIVE OIL
- VEGETABLE OIL

DESSERT
- 2 WHOLE EGGS
- 2 EGG YOLKS
- 30 ML CASTER SUGAR
- 10 ML NESCAFE GOLD BLEND
- 150 ML DOUBLE CREAM
- 300 ML STRONG BLACK COFFEE
- 150 ML MILD YOGHURT
- 40 G BITTER CHOCOLATE

ARMANDO, RENÉ, GILVLIANO, MATT, TSEYE, DAN & FIONA

atlantic

OPENING HOURS
MON–FRI 12.00-14.45 & 18.00-23.30,
SAT 18.00-23.30, SUN 19.00-22.00

CREDIT CARDS
VISA, MASTERCARD, AMEX, DINERS CLUB

When Oliver Peyton first discovered the cavernous rooms beneath the Regent Palace hotel, he must have felt as if he'd stumbled onto a gold mine. A painstaking, meticulous and no doubt costly renovation resulted in the stunning Atlantic bar and grill opening in 1994. The place is a temple to twenties elegance. The main room houses a big bar and a bigger restaurant, both dwarfed under the enormous ceilings. The adjoining 'Dick's bar' is named after legendary London barman, Dick Bradsall the original 'mixologist'. You'll find fabulous cocktails and globally influenced, dependable food in spectacular surroundings. Lunch is always a good bet at the Atlantic, offering a chance to absorb the Deco ambience, without the evening's soundtrack of a thousand exploding champagne corks.

roasted sweet butternut squash risotto with new season violetta garlic and coriander

In a hot pan, lightly colour the de-seeded and diced (1cm cubes) butternut squash, just softening. Then transfer to a rack and allow to cool. Pour the stock into a saucepan and bring to the boil. Reduce the heat so that the stock barely simmers. In another saucepan, heat the oil over a medium flame. Add the finely sliced onion, chopped garlic and cinnamon. Sauté gently without colour until softened, (around 3-5 minutes). Add the rice, stirring so as it is thoroughly coated in the oil and the edges of the rice become translucent. Add a ladleful of the simmering stock and continue stirring over a medium heat. When the stock has almost fully absorbed, add more, stirring to prevent the rice sticking. Do this until all the stock has absorbed. The risotto is done when the rice is tender but firm, (around 20 minutes). Add the butternut squash, freshly grated Parmesan and roughly chopped coriander, season to taste and serve immediately.

MAIN COURSE

- 500 G BUTTERNUT SQUASH
- 1 LITRE VEGETABLE STOCK
- 1/4 CUP OF VIRGIN OLIVE OIL
- 5 CLOVES OF VIOLETTA GARLIC
- 1/4 TEASPOON GROUND CINNAMON
- 1/2 BUNCH FRESH CORIANDER
- FRESHLY GROUND BLACK PEPPER
- 400 G RISOTTO RICE
- 1/2 CUP PARMESAN
- 1 LARGE ONION
- MALDON SEA SALT

orecchiette with roasted sweet cherry vine tomato and chorizo

Warm the olive oil in a large pan on a medium/low heat. Cut the chorizo into dices of 1 cm and add to the oil. Cook slowly until it is lightly golden brown and has become transparent. Hull the tomatoes and cut them into halves. Add the tomatoes, finely chopped garlic and coarsely chopped basil. Raise the heat to medium and cook, uncovered, until the tomatoes have softened, (usually around 5-6 minutes). Stir in the cream and simmer briefly until the liquid starts to thicken. Season and remove from the heat. Meanwhile, bring a large pot of salted water to the boil and add a little olive oil. Add the pasta and cook until tender, but firm to the bite. Whilst the pasta is cooking, re-heat the sauce gently. Drain the pasta and return to the warm pot. Lightly drizzle with olive oil and season. Add the sauce and toss until mixed. Divide into portions, garnish with a sprinkle of freshly grated Parmesan and serve.

MAIN COURSE

- 375 G CHORIZO
- 1/4 TEASPOON CELERY SALT
- 500 G CHERRY VINE TOMATOES
- 1 BUNCH BASIL
- 30 ML EXTRA VIRGIN OLIVE OIL
- 5 CLOVES OF NEW SEASON GARLIC
- 1 CUP DOUBLE CREAM
- MALDON SEA SALT
- FRESHLY GRATED BLACK PEPPER
- 500 G ORECCIETTE PASTA
- 1/2 CUP PARMESAN, FRESHLY GRATED

IBRAHIM, RICHARD & JAMES

bah humbug

OPENING HOURS
MON-FRI 17.00-24.00, SAT 11.00-24.00, SUN 11.00-23.30

CREDIT CARDS
VISA, MASTERCARD, DINERS CLUB

In the heart of Brixton, slap bang under St Mathew's Church, lurks Bah Humbug. The still functioning church's crypt has been given over and converted into this Modern international fish and vegetarian restaurant. Swathes of velvet, wrought iron and dripping candle wax adorn this subterranean eatery, creating a low lit, gothic air. Cyd Parker has created a menu that aims to offer a decent alternative to what can often be rather bland 'health obsessed' vegetarian fare. So, you'll find dishes like crispy Cantonese mock duck, or Wellington of mixed nuts, mushroom pâté and vege-tarian bacon, to tempt you, as well as a number of interesting fish choices. Next door, Humbug's sibling 'Bug bar', offers a club atmosphere in similarly 'spooky' surroundings.

thai seafood cocktail

"A 70S' REVIVAL WITH AN ORIENTAL TWIST"

Combine all the ingredients (finely chopped, if necessary) except the lettuce. Carefully mix together and refrigerate. Place the chopped lettuce in a bowl, then the other ingredients on top. Garnish with lemon and lime wedges, a dusting of paprika and a sprig of coriander.

WINE SUGGESTION DRY CHAMPAGNE, PERRIER JOUET BELLA POP

chocolate and hazelnut brûlée

"IT'S A REALLY CREAMY BRÛLÉE WITH A SURPRISE AT THE BOTTOM"

Beat the yolks and caster sugar together until it is thick. Bring the cream and vanilla pod to the boil, remove the pod and scrape the seeds into the mix. Mix the cream into the eggs and sugar, then return to the heat in a clean pan. Cook on a low heat until thickened, stirring constantly. Do not boil! Put the crushed nuts, brown sugar, water and cocoa powder into a pan. Heat until caramelised, add the butter at the end and mix in well. Divide the hazelnut mixture between 4 ramekins, top with the brûlée mixture and chill. Before serving, dust with brown sugar, spray with water and glaze with a blowtorch or under a very hot grill.

SERVE WITH APPLETON'S 5 YEAR OLD RUM, JAMAICA

STARTER

- 1 STICK LEMONGRASS
- 1 KAFFIR LIME LEAF
- 1 RED CHILLI
- 1 TABLESPOON CORIANDER
- 1/4 TEASPOON GALENGAL (THAI GINGER)
- 2 TABLESPOONS MAYONNAISE
- 2 TEASPOONS TOMATO KETCHUP
- JUICE OF 1/2 LIME
- 1/4 TEASPOON GREEN THAI CURRY PASTE
- SPLASH OF CHINESE FISH SAUCE
- 1 FRESH DRESSED CRAB FLESH
- 400 G PEELED PRAWNS
- FEW SPRIGS CORIANDER
- BLACK PEPPER
- COS LETTUCE
- 1 LEMON
- 1 LIME
- PAPRIKA

DESSERT

- 4 EGG YOLKS
- 30 G CASTER SUGAR
- 250 ML DOUBLE CREAM
- 1 VANILLA POD
- 100 G HAZELNUTS
- 50 G BROWN SUGAR
- SPLASH OF WATER
- 2 TEASPOONS OF GREEN AND BLACK'S COCOA POWDER
- 25 G BUTTER

TAOFIK, JAMES & ZOUN

bam-bou

BAM-BOU 1 PERCY STREET LONDON W1 TEL 0207 323 9130

OPENING HOURS
MON-SAT 12.00-15.00 & 18.00-23.30

CREDIT CARDS
VISA, MASTERCARD, AMEX, DINERS CLUB

Up in Fitzrovia, a tiny corner of the old French-Vietnamese colonial empire remains - in the shape of Bam-Bou. Spread over four floors of a grade 1 listed building, this beautifully decorated restaurant has cut no corners to achieve the desired effect. Lacquered walls; woven woodwork; silk screens and exotic fauna abound throughout its three dining rooms and lounges. In this rather serene setting, enjoy a pre-dinner cocktail before sampling some of chef Mark Read's fine Vietnamese dishes. This is delicate, fragrant food, made with contrasting textures and flavours. Upstairs are private dining rooms; and on a humid summers day you can fake the old spirit of Hanoi, on the small pavement veranda.

44

pork and pineapple stir-fry

Finely chop the garlic, shallots and ginger, then combine with the sugar and oyster sauce. Trim and slice the pork into nine thin slices. Marinate on a tray and add to the garlic/ginger mixture. Wash and slice the mushrooms, cut the mange tout into squares and shred the spring onions and pak choy. Combine all four. Skin and slice the pineapple into thick wedges. Fry the pork in a hot wok until 3/4 cooked. Add the vegetables and sauté. Add the pineapple and allow to cook until just soft. Serve immediately.

WINE SUGGESTION PINOT GRIS

bitter chocolate and pickled ginger mousse

"IT MAKES FOR A TASTY ALTERNATIVE TO CHOCOLATE MOUSSE"

Melt the chocolate and cream in a bain-marie over a medium heat until the chocolate dissolves. Add the egg, cocoa powder and sugar. Stir until the sugar dissolves. Blend in the chopped ginger and allow to cool. Whisk the egg white until stiff, then fold into the chocolate mixture. Pour the cooled mixture into a 3 cm diameter x 3.5 cm high cake ring. Cling film the base to avoid the mixture leaking. Refrigerate for 1 hour before slicing and serving.

SERVE WITH A SPOONFUL OF CRÈME FRAÎCHE
WINE SUGGESTION SWEET DESSERT WINE

MAIN COURSE
- 2 CLOVES OF GARLIC
- 2 SHALLOTS
- 1 STEM GINGER
- 2 TABLESPOONS CASTER SUGAR
- 2 TABLESPOONS OYSTER SAUCE
- 600 G PORK LOIN
- 500 G BUTTON MUSHROOMS
- 500 G MANGE TOUT
- 1 BUNCH SPRING ONION
- 4 HEADS PAK CHOY
- 1 SMALL PINEAPPLE

DESSERT
- 150 G PLAIN CHOCOLATE
- 200 ML DOUBLE CREAM
- 1 LARGE FREE-RANGE EGG
- 10 G COCOA POWDER
- 20 G CASTER SUGAR
- 30 G EGG WHITE
- 40 G PINK GINGER

CRAIG

beach blanket babylon

OPENING HOURS
LUNCH: MON-FRI 12.00-15.00,
SAT & SUN 12.00-17.00,
DINNER: SUN-THU 19.00-22.30,
FRI & SAT 19.00-23.30

CREDIT CARDS
VISA, MASTERCARD, AMEX, DINERS CLUB

Like a Gaudi fantasy, Beach Blanket Babylon weaves itself around two floors. Mosaic tiles, nooks and crannies, spiral stairs and labyrinthine cellars abound. The ground floor bar offers a fine line in cocktails, which can be taken on the terrace during summer months and by roaring open, stone clad, fires in winter. Descending into the gothic dining areas and you feel as if you've stepped into the vaults of a Transylvanian castle. The food is mostly Mediter-ranean, often leaning towards fish. Sets, as well as cartè menus are offered, along with a fairly decent wine list. A great space for decadent dining, holed up amongst the flickering lights and shadowy stone walls.

thai prawn curry

Sauté the peeled and diced butternut squash until golden. Leave to cool. Sauté the prawns in a little oil, add the curry paste and coconut milk, stir and bring to a simmer. Add the butternut squash, squeeze over the juice of the lime, add the fish sauce to taste, and the chopped basil. Serve.

SERVE WITH JASMINE RICE

• 1/2 BUTTERNUT SQUASH

• 35 PEELED TIGER PRAWNS

• VEGETABLE OIL

• 70 G THAI CURRY PASTE

• 11/2 SMALL TINS COCONUT MILK

• 11/2 LIMES

• FISH SAUCE

• 1/2 BUNCH BASIL

nanaimo bars

For the base, melt the chocolate, broken into small pieces, and butter together in a medium bowl, placed over a pan of simmering water. Remove bowl and stir in the biscuit crumbs and the roughly chopped hazelnut. Tip mixture into a baking tin, cover and refrigerate for 30 minutes. For the filling, put the egg yolk and milk in a heatproof bowl placed over a pan of barely simmering water, making sure the bowl does not touch the water. Whisk them together until warm to the touch. Remove bowl and constantly whisking and add the butter, vanilla essence. When it is fluffy, slowly add the sifted icing sugar. When it is fully incorporated, spread mixture over the base and chill for a further 30 minutes. For the topping, melt the chocolate and oil together as before. Allow to cool slightly, then spread over the filling quickly and evenly. Refrigerate again for at least 2 hours before serving.

DESSERT

LARGE BATCH

• 750 G DELUXE BELGIAN DARK CHOCOLATE

• 600 G UNSALTED BUTTER

• 600 G DIGESTIVE BISCUITS

• 600 G HAZELNUTS

• 8 LARGE EGG YOLKS

• 8 TABLESPOONS MILK

• 760 G UNSALTED BUTTER

• 8 TEASPOONS VANILLA ESSENCE

• 500 G ICING SUGAR

• 900 G DELUXE BELGIAN DARK CHOCOLATE

• 4 TABLESPOONS GROUNDNUT OIL

blue elephant

THE BLUE ELEPHANT 3-6 FULHAM BROADWAY LONDON SW6   TEL 0207 385 6595

OPENING HOURS
LUNCH: MON-SAT 12.00-14.30,
SUN 12.00-15.00,
DINNER: MON-FRI 19.00-00.30,
SAT 18.30-00.30, SUN 19.00-22.30

CREDIT CARDS
VISA, MASTERCARD, AMEX, DINERS CLUB

There are Thai restaurants and then there is the Blue Elephant. Step into this Fulham temple to Royal Thai cuisine and you enter a haven of trickling water, fresh Orchids, little wooden bridges, calm and serenity - The ideal environment to enjoy some truly exceptional Thai food. With branches across the world, they maintain a standard of service, ambience and cuisine that befits their global status as leaders of the field. A long and diverse menu, offers all your familiar favorites, along with a host of more obscure dishes. Its combination of top-notch food, fantastic surroundings and impeccable service, make for a very special outing. Recipes taken from The Blue Elephant cookbook, published by Pavilion.

thai fish cakes

Grind or process the fish and the squid into a smooth paste. Mix the curry paste, fish sauce, and sugar into the fish mixture. Add the kaffir lime leaves and French beans, which are cut into 2 mm slices. Fold in the beaten egg. Form 8 balls, using about 50 g of the mixture for each one. Flatten them into discs of about 5 mm thick and 6 cm in diameter. Deep fry in the vegetable oil, heated to 180°C, for 3 minutes. Remove the fishcakes from the oil and drain them on kitchen paper. Place on a bed of salad and sprinkle with the crushed and roasted peanuts. Serve the cucumber separately in a bowl.

STARTER

- 200 G FILLET OF COD OR OTHER WHITE FISH
- 200 G SQUID
- 2 1/2 TABLESPOONS RED CURRY PASTE
- 1 TABLESPOON FISH SAUCE
- 2 TEASPOONS SUGAR
- 2 KAFFIR LIME LEAVES
- 60 G FRENCH BEANS
- 1/2 EGG
- VEGETABLE OIL FOR DEEP-FRYING
- MIXED SALAD LEAVES
- 1/2 TEASPOON PEANUTS
- CUCUMBER TO SERVE

salmon soufflé

Soak the sticky rice in cold water for 30 minutes then pound into a paste. Pound the garlic, chilli, galangal and lemongrass and mix with the rice. Cut the salmon into fingers of about 7 cm long without removing any skin. Then gently mix them in a bowl with the pounded ingredients, adding the coconut milk, fish sauce, red curry paste and sugar. Stir in the finely sliced shallots, the coarsely chopped dill and lemon basil, taking care not to break up the salmon. Cut 4 oval shapes about 24 cm long x 16 cm wide, and 4 rectangles of about 12 cm x 8 cm from the banana leaf. Also cut a strip of about 27 cm long and 1 1/2 cm wide. Place the rectangles lengthways over the ovals to give two layers of leaf in the centre. Place a 1/4 of the mixture in the centre of each of the rectangles. Make a parcel with the banana leaf, and fasten it at the top with the thin banana strip and a toothpick. Bring a pan of water or a steamer to a fast boil and steam for 12 minutes. Serve hot.

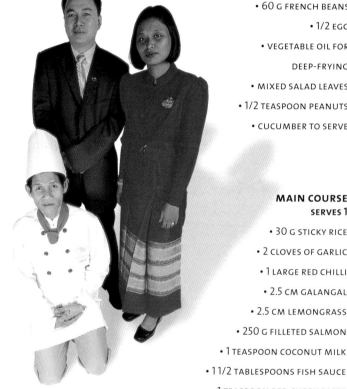

MAIN COURSE
SERVES 1

- 30 G STICKY RICE
- 2 CLOVES OF GARLIC
- 1 LARGE RED CHILLI
- 2.5 CM GALANGAL
- 2.5 CM LEMONGRASS
- 250 G FILLETED SALMON
- 1 TEASPOON COCONUT MILK
- 1 1/2 TABLESPOONS FISH SAUCE
- 1 TEASPOON RED CURRY PASTE
- 1 TEASPOON SUGAR
- 2 SHALLOTS
- 5 STEMS DILL
- 10 LEMON BASIL LEAVES
- 1 BANANA LEAF
- 4 TOOTHPICKS

PHOUTHONE, SOMLUCK & WISIT

cantaloupe

CANTALOUPE 35 CHARLOTTE ROAD LONDON EC3 TEL 0207 613 4411

OPENING HOURS
MON-FRI 12.30-15.00 & 18.30-23.00,
SAT 19.00-23.30

CREDIT CARDS
VISA, MASTERCARD, AMEX, DINERS CLUB

Years spent in the restaurant and bar business gave Richard Bigg and Nigel Foster a perfect vision of the sort of place they'd open given half the chance. That chance came with finding the ideal warehouse premises in a then forgotten corner of East London and Cantaloupe was born. The large airy bar and restaurant have a distinct downtown New York feel to them. Reclaimed brick and woodwork, mismatch chairs and chesterfield sofas add to the laid back vibe in the bar, where tapas are served all day. Out the back, the raised dining area presents a more refined, but no less funky feel. Chef Henry Brereton has been with the place almost from the start. His passion for fresh ingredients and fusing European and African cuisines shines through every mouthful.

roast cod wrapped in smoked paprika pancetta with spinach and cumin lentils

Remove the skin from cod and cut into 4 pieces. Wrap 2 pieces of pancetta around each piece and set aside. Rinse lentils, bring to the boil with the stock and simmer gently until lentils have absorbed all the liquid. Sweat down the finely diced vegetables and garlic with butter and a little olive oil. Add the cumin powder and cook for a further 2 minutes on a low heat. Add them to the lentils and chopped herbs - keep warm. Preheat a pan with butter and oil and add the cod. Roast on a medium heat for 10-15 minutes. Remove from oven and remove the cod from pan. Add spinach, salt and pepper to the pan's juices and cook on a high heat. Place the lentils on the bottom of the plate, followed by the spinach, then the cod.

MAIN COURSE

- 500 G COD FILLET, THICK CUT
- 8 THIN SLICES CURED SMOKED PAPRIKA PANCETTA
- 150 G PARDINA LENTILS
- 200 ML CHICKEN STOCK
- 50 G CARROTS
- 50 G LEEKS
- 50 G CELERY
- 50 G ONION
- 1 CLOVE OF GARLIC
- 50 G BUTTER
- OLIVE OIL
- 3 LARGE TABLESPOONS CUMIN POWDER
- 1/2 BUNCH CORIANDER
- 1/2 BUNCH FLAT LEAF PARSLEY
- 2 LARGE HANDFULS SPINACH
- SALT AND PEPPER

SANDRA, HENRY & CAT

dark chocolate cake

Melt the chocolate and butter together. Whisk the yolks with half the sugar. Whisk the whites with the remaining sugar. Add the chocolate and butter to the yolks. Fold in the almonds Fold in the egg whites and mix altogether. Add the mixture to a greased and floured 20 cm spring form and bake for 1-1 1/4 hours, at 165 °C.

DESSERT

- 250 G DARK CHOCOLATE COUVETURE
- 250 G BUTTER
- 8 EGGS
- 250 G CASTER SUGAR
- 250 G GROUND ALMONDS

caravaggio

CARAVAGGIO 107-112 LEADENHALL STREET LONDON EC3 TEL 0207 581 2366

OPENING HOURS
MON-FRI 11.45-15.00 & 18.00-22.00

CREDIT CARDS
VISA, MASTERCARD, AMEX, DINERS CLUB

Caravaggio occupies a former bank, right in the heart of the square mile. It's lofty interior has been split into two levels effectively creating two dining rooms in one space. The menu was overseen by the near legendary Alberico Penati of Harry's Bar, the member's only temple to Italian cuisine; and the kitchen headed by Jonathan Lees. With that in mind, you can expect a well-balanced menu of fine, authentic dishes. The city slickers, that make up a large proportion of the client base, obviously enjoy their meat, as there are is a good selection of richly flavoured veal, rabbit, beef and chicken dishes. Pasta and risotto are well covered and assuredly executed. The wine list goes from the modestly priced to off the Richter scale, but you'll find a grand selection, whatever the size of your pocket.

layered aubergines and sea-scallops with marina sauce

First prepare the sauce. Add to a large pan, a knob of butter and the finely chopped shallots. Gently fry, not letting them brown. Add the anchovy fillets, a little of the anchovy oil and the chopped tin-tomatoes. Cook until most of the moisture has evaporated. Liquidize and keep to one side. Cut the aubergine into approximately 5 mm thick slices. You will require 3 slices per portion. Either sauté or grill them for around 1 minute per side. Heat a little oil in a frying pan and sauté the scallops along with the basil and thyme, until they are golden. Place the scallops in the sauce and add the fresh tomatoes (peeled and deseeded.) Next, layer the aubergines and scallops with a little of the sauce. Put the remaining sauce on the plate, with the aubergine/scallop layers on top. Garnish with deep fried onion rings, cooked at 140°C.

SERVE WITH FRENCH BEANS AND POTATO PUREE
WINE SUGGESTION TOCAI '98, BORGO SAN DANIELLE, FRIULI

MAIN COURSE

- KNOB OF BUTTER
- 2 SHALLOTS
- 2-3 ANCHOVY FILLETS
- 1 TIN PLUM TOMATOES
- 2 LARGE AUBERGINES
- OLIVE OIL
- 16 KING SCALLOPS
- 2 LARGE ONIONS
- A FEW BASIL LEAVES
- A FEW SPRIGS OF THYME
- 6 FRESH PLUM TOMATOES
- DEEP FRIED ONION RINGS

italian chocolate and amaretto pudding with bitter chocolate sauce

"THIS CAN BE MADE IN ADVANCE AND SERVED AT ROOM TEMPERATURE WHEN REQUIRED"

First mix the eggs, sugar, crushed biscuits and cacao together in a bowl. In a saucepan bring the milk and cream to the boil. Pour over the egg mixture, stirring continuously. Pour the mix into individual pudding moulds and cook in a bain-marie at 180°C for 30 minutes. Meanwhile make the sauce. Put the chocolate and cream together in a bowl and place it over a pot of boiling water. Slowly melt them down, and keep slightly warm. Add amaretto to taste. Turn the puddings out and serve each with a drizzle of chocolate sauce.

WINE SUGGESTION MARSALA RISERVA FLORO, SICILIA

DESSERT

- 2 EGGS
- 60 G SUGAR
- 50 G AMARETTO BISCUITS
- 125 G MILK
- 125 G DOUBLE CREAM
- 50 G CACAO

FOR THE CHOCOLATE SAUCE

- 60 G BITTER CHOCOLATE
- 75 G WHIPPING CREAM
- AMARETTO LIQUOR TO TASTED

EMILIJA & SUSANA

che

OPENING HOURS
LUNCH: MON-FRI 12.00-15.00,
DINNER: MON-SAT 17.30-23.30

CREDIT CARDS
VISA, MASTERCARD, AMEX, DINERS CLUB

Converted from London's first listed 1960's building, Che is sleek and utterly chic. From the mosaic-clad lobby, you reach the first floor restaurant by a narrow, wood panelled escalator. A conscious decision was been made by owner Hani Farsi to provide a spacious, uncluttered feel to the dining area, and the temptation to cram a good few more tables in has been wisely resisted. Sit here enjoying Adam Gray's 'global fusion' cuisine, from carpaccio to curry. You'll overlook one of London's plushest areas, whilst being overlooked by Warhol's Marylin's. Take a post dinner tequila downstairs in the equally urbane bar; or for the truly decadent choose from one of thousands of Cuba's finest, in the low-slung leather clad Cigar lounge.

braised turbot with champagne and herb noodles

"CHEF'S FAVOURITE DISH"

Slice the shallots and mushrooms. Cook in a little butter until soft. Add the fish stock, bring to the boil and remove from heat. Seal the turbot fillets in a little oil until golden brown on each side. Remove and place in the fish stock at 180°C for eight minutes until just tender. Remove the fillets and pass the stock through a fine sieve into another pan. Cook the noodles 'al-dente' in salted boiling water. Remove and place in a pan with the melted butter, chopped chives and chervil. Bring the fish stock to the boil, add the double cream and slowly add the butter 10 g at a time until a smooth butter sauce has been achieved. Season with salt en pepper. Roll the noodles tightly around a serving fork forming four bundles. Put one bundle in a shallow bowl, placing the fish on one side. Add the champagne or sparkling wine to the sauce and spoon over the fish.

WINE SUGGESTION '96 SCOTCHMAN'S HILL, AUSTRALIA CHARDONNAY

MAIN COURSE

- 100 G SHALLOTS
- 100 G WHITE BUTTON MUSHROOMS
- 300 ML FISH STOCK
- 4 x 160 G TURBOT FILLETS
- 150 ML OLIVE OIL
- 350 G FRESH PASTA NOODLES
- 200 G UNSALTED BUTTER
- 1/4 BUNCH CHIVES
- 1/4 BUNCH CHERVIL
- 100 ML DOUBLE CREAM
- 200 ML CHAMPAGNE OR SPARKLING WINE
- SALT AND PEPPER

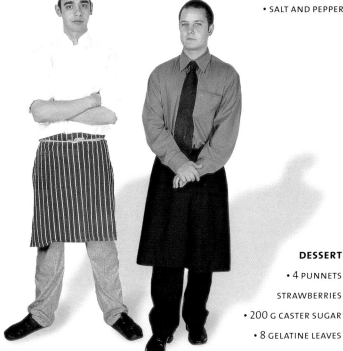

strawberry jelly with iced yoghurt

"IT'S A FRESH DESSERT, MAXIMISING THE STRAWBERRY FLAVOUR"

Cut 3 punnets of strawberries in half and place in a mixing bowl with the sugar. Cover with cling film. Place the bowl over a pan of boiling water for around 1 hour, until the strawberries are soft. Drain them through muslin cloth until all the juice has been extracted. Soak the gelatine leaves until soft and resolve in a little boiling water. Add to the strawberry juice. When at room temperature, pour the jelly into 4 cocktail glasses and place in the fridge for 2 hours. Finely dice the remaining strawberries and mix with some chopped mint, leaving to one side to infuse. Mix the sugar syrup (1:2 water to sugar, boiled and cooled) with the yoghurt and churn in an ice-cream maker. Place the diced strawberries on top of the jelly with a scoop of the sorbet yoghurt. Top with a sprig of mint.

WINE SUGGESTION '93 LA CHAPELL DE LA FLEURIE (SWEET)

DESSERT

- 4 PUNNETS STRAWBERRIES
- 200 G CASTER SUGAR
- 8 GELATINE LEAVES
- LITTLE WATER
- 1/4 BUNCH FRESH MINT
- 200 G NATURAL YOGHURT
- 400 ML SUGAR SYRUP

ALVARO & MARK

chez bruce

CHEZ BRUCE 2 BELLEVUE ROAD LONDON SW17 TEL 0208 672 0114

OPENING HOURS

MON–FRI 12.00-14.00 & 19.00-22.15,
SAT 12.30-14.30 & 19.00-22.30,
SUN 12.30-15.00

CREDIT CARDS

VISA, MASTERCARD, AMEX, DINERS CLUB

Bruce Poole has one more than one occasion been described as the chef's chef - The man who's cooking most other London chefs like to eat. Non-plussed by such praise, he continues to serve up unpretentious, intensely flavoured, classic French cuisine. 1999 saw Chez Bruce finally garnering a much-deserved Michelin star. Particularly popular are the set menus, where sampling this standard of cooking can be done for very reasonable prices. Found in a quiet corner of South-West London, overlooking Wandsworth common, Chez Bruce pulls the crowds for lunch and dinner six days a week, plus Sunday lunch. So be sure to book well ahead as distance is no object when it comes to a restaurant of this calibre.

tartare of mackerel with smoked salmon, crème fraîche and caviar

"IT'S A SIMPLE, QUICK AND EASY STARTER
WITH ELEGANT RESULTS"

Chop up the filleted, boned and skinned mackerel into very small dices and season with salt, cayenne pepper and lemon juice. Stir in the finely chopped chives and shallot. Place a portion on each slice of smoked salmon.

SERVE WITH A SPOONFUL EACH OF CRÈME FRAÎCHE AND CAVIAR.
WINE SUGGESTION PREMIER OR GRAND CRU CHABLIS

STARTER
- 4 LARGE, THIN SLICES OF SMOKED SALMON
- 4 MACKEREL
- CAYENNE PEPPER
- 1 LEMON
- CHIVES
- 1 SHALLOT
- 1 SMALL TUB CRÈME FRAÎCHE
- 50 G CAVIAR
- SALT

roast cod with olive oil mash

"IT'S PERFECT FOR A HOT SUMMERS DAY AS WELL AS
A COLD WINTERS NIGHT - NEVER OFF MY MENU"

Boil the potatoes, and make a smooth mash with milk, cream and plenty of olive oil. Roast the cod in a very hot pan, first over a high flame, until coloured, then at the bottom of a very hot oven. For the gremolate grate the lemon and mix with the very finely chopped garlic and parsley to form a dry, 'sprinkleable' consistency. Heat the mash, adding more oil if necessary, or if too oily a little more milk. Plate up the potato first. Top with the crisp, golden cod, then the tomato and a spoonful of the gremolata.

SERVE WITH A PLATE OF SPINACH AND ROASTED TOMATOES
(ROASTED WITH HERBS DE PROVENCE)
WINE SUGGESTION A BIG BUTTERY, OAK SOAKED CHARDONNAY

MAIN COURSE
- 800 G POTATOES
- A LITTLE MILK
- A LITTLE CREAM
- EXTRA VIRGIN OLIVE OIL
- 4 X 225 G PORTIONS OF VERY FRESH COD
- 1 LEMON
- 1 CLOVE OF GARLIC
- 2 TABLESPOONS PARSLEY

GRAHAM, MICHAEL, JOSE, VALERIE & ANTONIO

chutney mary

OPENING HOURS
MON-THU 12.30-14.30 & 19.00-23.30,
FRI & SAT 12.30-14.30 & 18.30-23.30,
SUN 12.30-15.00 & 19.00-22.30

CREDIT CARDS
VISA, MASTERCARD, AMEX, DINERS CLUB

Since 1990, when it opened, Chutney Mary has pioneered the new Indian cuisine philosophy. Its colonial 20's décor may hark back to a bygone age, but its food is firmly rooted in the present. Co-owner and executive head chef Namita Panjabi has literally travelled the length and breadth of her homeland sourcing original and, most importantly, authentic Indian recipes. Five different chefs man the kitchen, whose expertise provides a true taste of that vast region. Twice winner of 'The good Curry guide - best Indian restaurant award', most recently in 1999, this really is a leader of its field. Service is impeccable; and the ambience, especially the vaulted, verdant conservatory is an oasis of calm and refinement.

calamari chilli fry with coconut

Clean the calamari and cut into 1 cm rings. Marinate the rings with salt, pepper and half the lime juice. Leave aside for at least _ an hour, ideally overnight in the fridge. Heat the oil to a medium heat. Sauté the finely chopped garlic, ginger, green chilli and onion until the onion is transparent and still white. Increase the heat and add the calamari and grated coconut and stir-fry for around 2 minutes. Remove from the heat, add the remaining lime juice and toss. Sprinkle with the coarsely chopped coriander. Serve immediately.

masala pork

Mix the marinade and rub well into the diced pork. Set aside for at least 2 hours, ideally overnight in the fridge. Heat the oil in a shallow pan and sauté the sliced onion over a medium heat for around 2 minutes. Add the chopped tomatoes and cook for a further 7 minutes, stirring occasionally. Add the salt. Add the pork and sauté for around 5 minutes, until it's browned. Add a cup of water and cook on a low flame until nearly cooked. Meanwhile mix the coriander, cumin, and pepper powders. Sprinkle over the pork and close the lid. When the pork is ready, mix the lemon juice into the pork.

STARTER

- 600 G CALAMARI
- 1/2 TEASPOON SALT
- 1/4 TEASPOON WHITE PEPPER
- 1 LIME
- 2 TABLESPOONS OIL
- 3 CLOVES OF GARLIC
- 1 ONION
- 1 GREEN CHILLI
- 2 CM X 1 CM PIECE GINGER
- 3 TABLESPOON FRESH COCONUT
- 1 TABLESPOON FRESH CORIANDER LEAVES AND STALKS

MAIN COURSE

- 1 TEASPOON CHILLI POWDER
- 1 TEASPOON CINNAMON POWDER
- 1 TABLESPOON CUMIN POWDER
- 1 TEASPOON TURMERIC POWDER
- 1 TEASPOON PRESSED GINGER
- 1 TEASPOON GARLIC POWDER
- 1 KG PORK
- 1 ONION
- 3 TOMATOES
- 2 TEASPOONS SALT
- VEGETABLE OIL
- 1 TABLESPOON CORIANDER POWDER
- 1/2 TEASPOON CUMIN POWDER
- 1/2 TEASPOON PEPPER POWDER
- 2 TABLESPOONS LEMON JUICE

EDDIE & MURRALI

cicada

CICADA 132 ST. JOHN'S STREET LONDON EC1 TEL 0207 608 1550

OPENING HOURS
MON-FRI 12.00-15.00 & 18.00-23.00,
SAT 18.00-23.00

CREDIT CARDS
VISA, MASTERCARD, AMEX, DINERS CLUB

'Pacific Fusion' is an ambiguous term and more often than not, Indian, Thai, Indonesian, even European influences will find their way into dishes, as well as the more strictly 'Pacific' elements. Geographic particulars aside; Cicada was one of the first to use the phrase, and still remains one of the best exponents of it. Dishes straddle many cultures and cooking styles, producing inventive and exciting hybrids. So, Tempura might turn up along side tapenade, sweet ginger with Tiramisu. Head chef Ian Pengelly has produced his particular 'cut and paste' style here for the last few years. The low lit, leather clad décor harmonizes perfectly with the laid back clientele, whose mixture of styles and fashions complement the menus perfectly.

chilli salt squid

STARTER

- 400 G SQUID
- 6 RED 'BIRDS-EYE' CHILLIES
- 50 G CORNFLOUR
- 3 SPRING ONIONS
- FOR THE SWEET CHILLI SAUCE
- 300 G SUGAR
- 200 ML RICE VINEGAR
- 1 BULB OF GARLIC
- 10 RED CHILLIES
- 50 ML FISH SAUCE
- OIL
- SALT

Score the cleaned squid in a criss-cross pattern and cut into 7 cm squares, using the tentacles too. Finely slice the chilli. Heat a little oil in a pan or wok. Dust the squid pieces in cornflour, shaking off any excess. Fry the squid in very hot oil, stirring once or twice to ensure no pieces stick together. Remove and drain well on kitchen towel. Combine the spring onion, sliced 'julienne', and chilli, toss in the squid and season with salt. To make the sweet chilli sauce, boil the sugar and vinegar together, add the bulb of garlic cut in half, and the de-seeded and blended chilli. Boil for a further 4-5 minutes, then add the fish sauce. Serve in paper cones with chopsticks, accompanied with the sweet chilli sauce.

sweet ginger tiramisu

In a medium bowl, over a pan of barely simmering water, whisk 130 ml of ginger wine, sugar, minced ginger stem, ginger syrup and ginger powder. Separate the eggs. Add the egg yolks and gently warm, not allowing eggs to scramble. Leave to cool. When it's cool, slowly add the mascarpone. In a separate bowl, whisk the egg whites until soft peaks form. Fold this into the mascarpone mix. Soak the cubed sponge in the remaining ginger wine and divide them into four small ramekins. Fill with the mascarpone mix, to half way. Add some crumbled meringue and spread some more mascarpone mix over, to form a level top. Refrigerate until set. Before serving, dust one half of each ramekin with icing sugar, and the other half with cocoa.

DESSERT

- 330 ML GINGER WINE
- 50 G SUGAR
- 2 STEM GINGERS
- 80 ML GINGER SYRUP
- 1 TEASPOON GINGER POWDER
- 2 EGGS
- 250 G MASCARPONE CHEESE
- 100 G SPONGE
- 4 MERINGUE NESTS
- 100 G ICING SUGAR
- 100 G COCAO

club gascon

OPENING HOURS
MON-FRI 12.00-14.30 & 19.00-22.00,
SAT 19.00-22.30

CREDIT CARDS
VISA, MASTERCARD

After an illustrious career cooking for some of the finest establishments of Paris, Versailles and St. Tropez, Pascal Aussignac was enticed across the water to head the kitchen at Club Gascon. Lucky us. His obsession and flair with French cuisine makes for wonderful eating. The menu is split into six sections including one devoted entirely to Foie Gras, listing eleven dishes. It breaks away from the standard three courses, with most people ordering four or five smaller plates, and allows for a much wider variety of tastes. Standing in the heart of Smithfield, Club Gascon's sleek interior, all dark blue velvet and marble is as appealing as its menu. Next doors equally swish bar leaves little doubt as to where to enjoy an after dinner digestive, or three.

roast monkfish, stewed beans and lavender

"THE LAVENDER TASTE IS UNUSUAL. IT'S A TYPICAL DISH OF SOUTHWEST FRANCE"

Soak the beans in warm water overnight. Mix the lavender flowers with the white wine vinegar and soy sauce and leave overnight. Put some butter or duck fat in a pan with the stock and water. Add some thyme, bay leaves and garlic to taste. Add the beans and cook slowly, for approximately 2 hours. When they are soft, they are ready. Pan fry the monkfish in butter or duck fat. Add the wine vinegar and soy sauce to the cooked beans. Pan-fry the spring onions. Assemble on a plate, first the beans, then monkfish and finally the spring onions on top of the fish.

WINE SUGGESTION MONTRAVEL WHITE

MAIN COURSE

- 320 G DRIED BEANS
- 1 BUNCH LAVENDER
- 500 ML WHITE WINE VINEGAR
- 2 TEASPOONS KIKKOMAN SOY SAUCE
- 100 G BUTTER OR DUCK FAT
- 250 G DUCK STOCK
- 250 G WATER
- SPRIG OF THYME
- 4 BAYLEAVES
- GARLIC
- 400 G FILLET MONKFISH
- 8 SPRING ONIONS

sweet foie gras with apple candy

"IN ROMAN TIMES, FOIE GRAS WAS ALWAYS EATEN IN DESSERT. THE COMBINATION WITH THE APPLE MAKES IT SWEET ENOUGH FOR MOST PEOPLES TASTE"

Boil the liquor, allow to cool and add the pâté. Marinade in the fridge for six hours. Peal all but one Granny Smiths (setting aside a large one), and cut them into 1/2 cm cubes. Sauté in clarified butter until caramelised. Deglaze the pan with the apple liquor marinade and put to one side. Slice the large apple paper thin, ideally in a processor. Place the slivers on a buttered baking tray, or silicon paper, and cook in the oven at 80°C for two hours until they are crisp and dry. Vacuum pack/seal in cling film the foie gras and steam for three minutes. Then slice it as thinly as possible. Serve with the caramelised apple, place the wafer apple on top and drizzle any remaining sauce around the plate.

SERVE WITH GREEN APPLE SPIRIT

DESSERT

- 1 BOTTLE APPLE LIQUOR
- 1 DUCK FOIE GRAS, EXTRA
- 5 GRANNY SMITH APPLES
- 30 G CLARIFIED BUTTER
- 30 G SUGAR

PASCAL

il convivio

OPENING HOURS
MON-SAT 12.00-15.00 & 19.00-23.00

CREDIT CARDS
VISA, MASTERCARD, AMEX, DINERS CLUB

In the refined environs of Belgravia you will find Il Convivio. Light and intimate, with an electric roof covered terrace, it offers fine quality Tuscan influenced Italian food. Chef Lukas Pfaff was born and bred in the distinctly un-Italian Black forest, where he first began cooking at his family's hotel. After stints at some of Germany and France's finest establishments he moved to London and began honing his skill for Italian cookery. Dishes are richly flavoured and immaculately presented. Home-made pasta is a particular speciality, such as black spaghetti with lobster and spring onions. The wine list offers one of the best selections of Italian wines in the city. There is also a delightful private dining room, offering a totally self-contained home away from home, without the washing up.

pasta 'stracci' with pesto sauce

"TYPICAL TUSCAN FOOD"

First make the pasta. Combine the flour, semolina, eggs and a little oil in a bowl. Mix together to form a fine blend. Using a pasta maker, roll out the pasta. Cut it into small 2.5 cm squares (dried pasta may be used). Next make the pesto by blending the basil, pine nuts, walnuts, garlic, grated Parmesan and olive oil. Set aside. Boil the French beans in salted water, remove when tender and set aside. Boil the potatoes in salted water then peel and halve them. Boil the pasta in a large pan of salted water with a little olive oil. 4-5 minutes for fresh, 8 minutes for dried. Combine the pesto, potatoes and beans in a large saucepan. Add the cooked pasta and heat very gently. Too much cooking will blacken the pesto. Turn out into a serving dish and garnish with fresh basil.

WINE SUGGESTION SAUVIGNON, VENICA '99

pan-fried skewers of monkfish

"IT'S QUICK, SIMPLE AND DELICIOUS"

Cut the filleted monkfish into 12 pieces. Peel the onions and cut it into 4 pieces and separate the layers. Cut the courgette and aubergine into 2.5 cm chunks. Trim 4 of the long rosemary stalks, leaving the tip. Using the stalk as a skewer, alternate the 3 vegetables and monkfish, until you have an even 'kebab'. Wash the rocket and place it on a flat dish. Fry the bacon until it is crispy. Panfry the monkfish skewers in olive oil with a clove of garlic until they are nicely coloured. Transfer the skewers into an oven at 200°C for 5-6 minutes. Remove from the oven and place the skewers on the rocket. Sprinkle with balsamic vinegar and top with the crispy bacon.

WINE SUGGESTION ASSOLO '97, VIGNETI MASSA

STARTER

- 250 G 00 FLOUR
- 100 G FINE SEMOLINA
- 3 WHOLE EGGS
- EXTRA VIRGIN OLIVE OIL
- 2 BUNCHES BASIL
- 50 G PINE NUTS
- 20 FRESH WALNUTS
- 2 CLOVES OF GARLIC
- 50 G PARMESAN CHEESE
- 200 ML EXTRA VIRGIN OLIVE OIL
- 125 G FINE FRENCH BEANS
- 10 NEW POTATOES
- SALT

MAIN COURSE

- 1 MEDIUM MONKFISH TAIL
- 2 RED ONIONS
- 1 COURGETTE
- 1 SMALL AUBERGINE
- 1 BUNCH LONG ROSEMARY
- LARGE BUNCH ROCKET
- 12 SLICES O STREAKY BACON
- OLIVE OIL FOR COOKING
- 1 CLOVE OF GARLIC
- 1 TABLESPOON BALSAMIC VINEGAR
- SALT AND PEPPER

ANDREA & LUCAS

the cow

THE COW 89 WESTBOURNE PARK ROAD LONDON W2 TEL 0207 221 0021

OPENING HOURS
MON-SAT 19.00-23.00, SUN 19.30-22.30

CREDIT CARDS
DINERS CLUB

Not so long ago the cow was a rather shabby little pub struggling to survive. Today it's a very different story. Owner Tom Conran proves he has his fathers Midas touch, giving the old place a total refit and new 'Irish' direction, and turning it's fortunes around. Downstairs in the saloon; a tiny brasserie, seafood counter and bar heave under the almost constant demands of its loyal crowd. Whilst upstairs you'll find the rather calmer dining room. Simply furnished with nine or ten tables, they produce a new menu daily. As with downstairs seafood features heavily, but there will always be a good few carnivorous alternatives. The wine list is relatively short, but most folks opt for a few pints of the black stuff - washes the oysters down a treat.

potted shrimp

Clarify the butter by putting the butter and mace in a double boiler (or bowl set over a pan of simmering water). As the butter melts, a white crust will form on the surface. Skim this off with a slotted spoon. Pour the butter through a sieve lined with muslin into a bowl. Add the peeled shrimp to the butter, season with a little salt and pepper and mix together. Pack the mixture into ramekins and refrigerate. Remove from fridge 1/2 and hour before serving to soften slightly.

SERVE WITH HOT BROWN TOAST AND WATERCRESS
WINE SUGGESTION SANCERRE

STARTER
- 125 G UNSALTED BUTTER
- 1 BLADE MACE OR 1/4 TEASPOON GROUND MACE
- 250 G GREY SHRIMP
- SALT AND PEPPER

seared tuna, courgette fritters and aioli

Make the aioli: beat together the egg yolks, finely crushed garlic and a little salt. Mix the two oils together and slowly add the oil, whisking it in a little at a time until the mixture is thick and all the oil is incorporated. Cut the courgette into 5 cm batons and put them in a colander and lightly sprinkle with salt, allow to drain for 1 hour. Beat the eggs together with the olive oil. Toss the courgettes in the flour (seasoned with black pepper), then dip them into the mixture of egg and oil, then back into the flour. Deep-fry them at 180°C until crisp and golden. Sear the tuna in a very hot pan for approximately 2 minutes each side. Serve the tuna and fritters with a dipping bowl of aioli and wedges of lemon.

SERVE WITH A GOOD, RIPE TOMATO SALAD
WINE SUGGESTION UN-OAKED CHARDONNAY

MAIN COURSE
- 2 EGG YOLKS
- 4 CLOVES OF GARLIC
- SALT
- 125 ML OLIVE OIL
- 125 ML SALAD OIL
- 8 COURGETTES
- 250 G PLAIN FLOUR
- BLACK PEPPER
- 2 EGGS
- 125 OLIVE OIL
- OIL FOR DEEP-FRYING
- 4 TUNA STEAKS
- 1 LEMON

SUSAN & IRENA

the eagle

THE EAGLE 159 FARRINGDON ROAD LONDON EC1 TEL 0207 837 1353

OPENING HOURS
MON-FRI 12.30-14.30 & 18.30-22.30,
SAT 12.30-15.30 & 18.30-22.30,
SUN 12.30-15.30

CREDIT CARDS
VISA, MASTERCARD

Back in the days when a pub meant stale tobacco, warm ale and a packet of peanuts the Eagle became something of a mould breaker. It was the first of what is now the norm - gastro pubs. Not much has changed since they put bruschetta alongside the bitter. The décor is un-pretentious, the clientele loyal and the food consistently good. Chef Tom Norrington-Davies serves up a Portuguese/Spanish hybrid. Good rustic, hearty food. Where so many of its imitators attempt to produce ever more complex menus, the Eagle's strength lies in the fact that it realizes exactly the sort of food that's suited to a pub environment. And mercifully, all served up without a 'theme' in sight.

chilled aubergine soup with yoghurt and paprika

"THIS IS A GREAT SUMMER SOUP. WE MAKE IT WHEN
WE ARE FED UP WITH GAZPACHO"

Char the aubergines over a naked flame until the skin is
blackened. Leave to cool completely. Sweat the finely chopped
onions and garlic in the olive oil until soft and translucent.
Remove from the heat and add the paprika. Remove the skin
from the aubergines and add the flesh to the onions. Add the
yoghurt. Transfer all the ingredients to a blender and mix
to a smooth puree. Dilute to the consistency required
with the cold stock. Season with salt and pepper
and a little lemon juice.

SERVE WITH GRILLED PEPPER OR CHOPPED
CORIANDER AS A GARNISH AND A COLD BEER

STARTER

- 2 LARGE AUBERGINES
- 2 MEDIUM ONIONS
- 2 CLOVES OF GARLIC
- 1 TABLESPOON EXTRA VIRGIN OLIVE OIL
- 1 TEASPOON SPANISH (SMOKED) PAPRIKA
- 300 ML GREEK YOGHURT
- 1 LITRE COLD VEGETABLE OR CHICKEN STOCK
- SALT AND PEPPER
- 1/2 LEMON

bife ana, portuguese rumpsteak sandwich

"THERE WOULD BE A RIOT IN CLERKENWELL IF
WE TOOK THIS OFF THE MENU"

Make the marinade: mix together the thinly sliced
onions, roughly chopped garlic, crushed chillies, roughly
chopped parsley, pepper, half the wine and the oil. Cut the
steak into thin strips and coat them thoroughly and leave to
marinade for around 2 hours. Cut the ciabbata into 4 hefty
sections and warm it in the oven. Cut into doorstep sandwiches
and line each with lettuce. Heat a large skillet until smoking
hot. Sear the steak, with marinade, for around 30 seconds
each side. Season with salt as you turn the meat over. Fill each
sandwich with the meat and marinade. Deglaze the pan with
the remaining wine and pour over the sandwiches.

SERVE WITH COLD LAGER

MAIN COURSE

- 2 LARGE ONIONS
- 3 CLOVES OF GARLIC
- 1/2 TABLESPOON DRIED CHILLIES
- 1 BUNCH FLAT LEAF PARSLEY
- 1/2 TABLESPOON BLACK PEPPER
- 1 GLASS RED WINE
- 4 TABLESPOONS OLIVE OIL
- 900 G RUMPSTEAK
- 1 CIABBATA LOAF
- 1/2 ICEBERG (OR SIMILAR) LETTUCE
- SALT

PABLO, STEPHANIE & MICHAEL

fish!

FISH! CATHEDRAL ST. BOROUGH MARKET LONDON SE1 TEL 0207 234 3333

OPENING HOURS
MON–SAT 11.30–15.00 & 17.30–23.00

CREDIT CARDS
VISA, MASTERCARD, AMEX, DINERS CLUB

Borough was until very recently a half forgotten slice of old London. Suddenly the area's exploded with the Tate Modern, 'wobbly bridge', Vinopolois and whole host of regeneration. FISH! sits slap bang in the middle of it all. As the name suggests it offers a menu almost exclusively based around 'the slippery ones'. On the placemat menu, there is a list of 23 different species, which are ticked daily according to availability. Your choice can be either grilled or steamed, and served with one of five sauces and vegetables. This is ultra fresh, simply cooked and reasonably priced fish, something that is surprisingly rare in this city. This branch was the first of what has now become a small chain, or should that be 'small shoal'?

smoked haddock and welsh rarebit

"THE UNUSUAL COMBINATION OF FISH AND
CHEESE IS VERY TASTY"

Put the milk and Guinness in a pan and gently warm.
Add the grated cheese and melt slowly until fondue,
(smooth and runny). Add the Worcestershire sauce
and mustard and mix. Add the flour and breadcrumbs
and cook out for 2 minutes on a gentle heat. Place
mixture into a mixer and slowly add the eggs and salt
and pepper. Sear the haddock fillet on both sides and
spread the mixture on top. Place under a medium grill
until golden brown.

SERVE WITH TOMATO AND BASIL SALAD,
OLIVE OIL AND SEA SALT
WINE SUGGESTION CHARDONNAY 'MONT ROSÉ'

- 50 ML MILK
- 50 ML GUINNESS
- 350 G CHEDDAR
- 40 ML WORCESTERSHIRE SAUCE
- 20 G ENGLISH MUSTARD
- 15 G FLOUR
- 40 G BREADCRUMBS
- 30 G EGG YOLK
- 1 WHOLE EGG
- SALT AND PEPPER
- 4 x 150 G HADDOCK FILLETS

fish pie

"IT'S A VERY SIMPLE RECIPE FOR A
TRADITIONAL CLASSIC DISH"

Cut the fish into 2.5 cm pieces. Quarter the
mushrooms and cook them briefly. Into a bowl add the
drained mushrooms, velouté, salt and pepper. Mix
together and place in an earthenware dish, spreading
mashed potatoes over the top. Cook for 15 minutes on
a medium/high heat. Remove from oven and sprinkle
the grated cheese on top. Place under a medium grill
until browned.

SERVE WITH CRISP GREEN SALAD
WINE SUGGESTION SAUVIGNON NORTON

MAIN COURSE

- 100 G COD OR ANY OTHER
  FIRM WHITE FISH
- 100 G SMOKED HADDOCK
- 100 G SALMON
- 100 G MUSHROOMS
- 500 ML FISH VELOUTÉ
- 2 G SALT
- 2 G PEPPER
- 300 G POTATOES
- 200 G CHEDDAR

CLAIRE

the glasshouse

OPENING HOURS
MON-SAT 12.00-14.30 & 19.00-22.30,
SUN 12.00-15.00

CREDIT CARDS
VISA, MASTERCARD, AMEX

Tucked away along a tiny Kew side street lies the Glasshouse. Because of its location you might expect a good neighbourhood type restaurant, which indeed it is. But the cooking is up there with the best of them. Co-owned by the exacting Mr. Bruce Poole (he of Chez Bruce), it couldn't really be any other way. Chef Anthony Boyd serves up a modern British menu, with Mediterranean inflections. The food is strong, richly flavoured and imaginatively devised. Expect dishes like fennel and shrimp risotto or braised beef, with horseradish mash and Madera jus. Deep flavours, perfectly executed. The cooking, along with a long and thoughtfully compiled wine list (with a good few half bottles), and attentive but by no means intrusive service, make this a very fine restaurant indeed.

baked hake with charlotte potatoes, spinach and crab bisque

"WHAT'S WRONG WITH HAKE?!"

Chop the crab bones and place into a roasting tray. Roast on at 200°C for 20 minutes. Remove the bones and add the chopped vegetables, herbs and tomato puree. Place back in the oven and roast for a further 10 minutes. Add the Pernod and stir. Place the bones back onto the vegetables, cover with water and cook on a medium stove for 15-20 minutes. Strain the liquid and return it to the heat. Reduce to taste. Set aside. Place the potatoes into a large pan and boil until tender. Place the hake fillets onto buttered ovenproof paper, season well and roast for 8-10 minutes at 170°C. Whilst this is cooking, boil the spinach. Arrange on the middle of plates in balls, with the sliced potatoes circling them. Bring the bisque back to the boil, add the cream, chives, lemon juice and seasoning. Pour over spinach and potatoes. Top with the hake and serve.

SERVE WITH ANY GREEN VEGETABLES
WINE SUGGESTION AU BON CLIMAT CHARDONNAY RESERVE BIEN NAUDO '97, CALIFORNIA

MAIN COURSE

- 2 KG CRAB BONES
- 1 CARROT
- 1/2 ONION
- 2 STICKS CELERY
- 1 LEEK
- BAYLEAF
- FEW BASIL LEAVES
- 100 G TOMATO PUREE
- 1/2 GLASS PERNOD
- 1 KG POTATOES
- 4 X 200 G HAKE FILLETS
- BUTTER
- SALT AND PEPPER
- 1 KG SPINACH
- 200 ML DOUBLE CREAM
- 1 BUNCH CHIVES
- 1/2 LEMON

ANTHONY & ANDRÉ

great eastern

GREAT EASTERN DINING ROOM 54-56 GREAT EASTERN STREET LONDON EC2 TEL 0207 613 4545

OPENING HOURS
MON-FRI 12.00-15.00 & 18.00-24.00,
SAT 18.00-24.00

CREDIT CARDS
VISA, MASTERCARD, AMEX, DINERS CLUB

Great eastern dining room has fed the hip and the beautiful denizens of Shoreditch since the beginning of its reinvention as cool capital. It's sleek dark wood interior with floor to ceiling caricatures, serves up modern Italian rustic grub. The upstairs is split into a spacious bar and a clean, uncluttered dining area, which overflows downstairs. The basement plays host to a free club most evenings, and as with most things in this neck of the woods, everything is done at a rather laid back pace. Prices are very reasonable; especially as you may well be munching your rocket and Parmesan seated next to the new 'Basquiet' - for that week at least.

pea, pancetta, broad bean and goat's cheese salad

"IT'S A GOOD SEASONAL SALAD, EASILY PREPARED AT HOME"

Cut the pancetta into lardoons and fry in a pan with no oil, until crispy. Place the beans and peas in boiling, salted water for 30 seconds. Drain and plunge into iced water. For the pesto - blend the basil, garlic, toasted pine nuts, Parmesan and oil until smooth. In a large bowl mix together the beans, pancetta, pesto and crumbled goat's cheese. Season and add a squeeze of lemon. Garnish with the herb sprigs.

SERVE WITH ROCKET

STARTER

- 150 G PANCETTA
- 160 G FRESH PEAS
- 80 G BROAD BEANS
- 1/2 BUNCH BASIL
- 1 BULB OF GARLIC
- 25 G PINE NUTS
- 50 G PARMESAN
- OLIVE OIL
- 100 G GOAT'S CHEESE
- SALT AND PEPPER
- 1/2 LEMON
- SPRIGS OF MINT
- SPRIGS OF PARSLEY
- A FEW PURPLE BASIL LEAVES
- SPRIGS OF TARRAGON

spaghetti vongole

Pre-cook the spaghetti 'al dente'. Rinse the clams under cold water. Cut the shallots, garlic and chilli into a fine dice and sweat in olive oil in a frying pan. Increase the heat, add the clams and wine. Cover the pan and cook until the clams open (around 1 minute). Add the spaghetti and toss through the clam mix. Season with salt and pepper, a squeeze of lemon and serve. Garnish with parsley.

MAIN COURSE

- 500 G SPAGHETTI
- 500 G CLAMS
- 2 BANANA SHALLOTS
- 1/2 CLOVE OF GARLIC
- 1/2 RED CHILLI
- 4 TABLESPOONS OLIVE OIL
- 100 ML WHITE WINE
- SALT AND PEPPER
- 1/2 LEMON
- 1/2 BUNCH FLAT LEAF PARSLEY

MICHAEL, EMMA & FRANCK

isola

ISOLA 145 KNIGHTSBRIDGE LONDON SW1 TEL 0207 838 1044

OPENING HOURS
ISOLA: MON-SAT 18.00-23.30,
OSTERIA: MON-SAT 12.00-14.30
& 18.00-23.30, SUN 12.00-15.30
& 18.00-22.30

CREDIT CARDS
VISA, MASTERCARD, AMEX, DINERS CLUB

Isola is really two restaurants in one. Downstairs is the simpler Osteria, described as rustic Italian cuisine, open for lunch and dinner. Upstairs is the altogether more serious 'gourmet Italian' Isola, which is a distinctly evening affair. The design is chic and so is the eating. Immaculately prepared and presented, although never too fussy, your food is served in fashionable surroundings and more than likely, fashionable company. Another of Mr. Peyton's outlets, it bears all the hallmarks of his fastidious and tasteful touch. Bruno Loubet controls the kitchen and is the man many diners hand over their trust to with his choice of the nightly gourmet menu. Discreet booths ensure no conversation is too indiscreet. Perfect for a spot of 'power-dining'.

red mullet stuffed with fennel and citrus zest, tomato and olive sauce

Bone the fish. Slice the fennel and cook it in olive oil without colouring. Add half of the chopped garlic and citrus zest. Mix well and set aside. In the same pan re-heat the remaining oil and cook the peeled and chopped tomatoes, the remaining garlic, thyme and olives. Season with salt and pepper and stew for 5 minutes. Stuff the mullet with the fennel and tie with string. Cook in a pan for about 8-10 minutes over a moderate heat. Add the spring onions a couple of minutes before removing from the heat. Pour the sauce onto a serving dish, place the fish on top and sprinkle with basil and other herbs of your choice.

fresh fruit in star anise syrup

Peel and cut the fruit. Boil the water with the sugar, star anis and the vanilla pod for 2 minutes. Leave to cool completely. Empty the passion fruit into a bowl and crush it together with 3 tablespoons of the above syrup. Crush the raspberries in a bowl then add 3 tablespoons of the syrup. Pour the remaining syrup over the other fruit. Dress the fruit on a plate and add the passion fruit sauce and raspberry sauce. Add a squeeze of lime. Finish with fresh mint and a biscuit of your choice.

SERVE WITH LIME SORBET

MAIN COURSE
- 5 X 250 G RED MULLET FILLETS
- 250 G FENNEL
- 100 ML OLIVE OIL
- 3 CLOVES OF GARLIC
- 1/2 ORANGE
- 1/2 LEMON
- 750 G TOMATOES
- 1/4 BUNCH FRESH THYME
- 75 G BLACK OLIVES
- SALT AND PEPPER
- 1 BUNCH SPRING ONIONS
- 1/4 BUNCH FRESH BASIL

DESSERT
- 5 KIWI FRUITS
- 3 ORANGES
- 2 GRAPEFRUIT
- 1/2 PINEAPPLE
- 1 MANGO
- 10 STRAWBERRIES
- 150 ML WATER
- 150 G SUGAR
- 3 STAR ANISE
- 1 VANILLA POD
- 2 PASSION FRUIT
- 40 RASPBERRIES
- 1 FRESH LIME
- 1/4 BUNCH FRESH MINT
- BISCUITS (BISCOTTI ARE RECOMMENDED)

BRUNO, LIONEL, GRAIG & DANIEL

kennington lane

KENNINGTON LANE 205 KENNINGTON LANE LONDON SE11 TEL 0207 793 8313

OPENING HOURS
MON-FRI 12.00-15.00 & 18.00-22.30,
SAT 18.00-22.30,
SUN 12.00-16.00 & 18.00-22.30

CREDIT CARDS
VISA, MASTERCARD, AMEX, DINERS CLUB

Pedigree, quality and ability, are key words for this impeccable eatery just south of the river. Chef Phillip Wooller has trained at, most notably, The Ritz and Mayfair's The Greenhouse, and at 29 is a name to watch. Manager Olivier Moudjeb is charm personified, not surprising for a man who's worked for the best, including Pierre-White and Ramsay. The commitment here is to offer a top-notch neighborhood restaurant for this rapidly growing area. Wooller's recipes bridge the best of French and Italian cuisine seamlessly. And on the rare occasion of some good weather appearing, all this can be enjoyed on the delightful terrace tucked away in the little courtyard to the rear.

potato pancake, smoked salmon, crème fraîche and caviar

"IT'S AN ABSOLUTE CLASSIC DISH AND HAS PROVEN TO BE
THE MOST POPULAR STARTER ON THE MENU"

First cook and mash the potatoes. Place the flour in the bowl, make a well in the centre and add the whole eggs. Gradually mix in the milk and cream. Whisk in the egg whites and add the mashed potato, freshly grated nutmeg and seasoning and whisk until smooth. Leave to rest for 30 minutes. Preheat the oven to 250°C. Heat a little oil in a blinis or small pan, pour in the pancake mix and place directly in the oven for 15 minutes. Turn out, top with a rosette of smoked salmon, crème fraîche, caviar and chopped chives.

WINE SUGGESTION PETIT CHABLIS DOM DU CHARDONNAY, FRANCE '98

STARTER
- 450 G FLOURY POTATOES
- 3 HEAPED TABLESPOONS OF SELF-RAISING FLOUR
- 3 EGGS
- 150 ML MILK
- 150 ML DOUBLE CREAM
- 2 EGG WHITES
- 1 TEASPOON NUTMEG
- SALT AND PEPPER
- 450 G SMOKED SALMON
- 100 G CRÈME FRAÎCHE
- 25 G CAVIAR
- CHIVES
- OIL

seared scallops, risotto nero and anchovy spinach

Melt half of the butter in a saucepan, add the chopped shallot and sweat for 2 minutes. Add the rice and cook for another 3 minutes. Add 25 ml of the Pernod and the star anise. Gradually add the hot fish stock and the squid ink at intervals. Stir frequently, adding more stock. The rice should take 20-25 minutes to cook. Finish with the remaining Pernod and butter. Season to taste. Fry the spinach, when cooked, add the anchovy. Season the scallops then fry in a hot pan until golden on both sides. Deglaze the pan with a little lemon juice. Stack the dishes, finishing with the lemon juice, poured over the scallops.

WINE SUGGESTION BERGERAC SEMILLION, CHATEAU LA TOUR DES JENDRES, FRANCE '98

MAIN COURSE
- 50 G BUTTER
- 1 SHALLOT
- 300 G RISOTTO RICE
- 50 ML PERNOD
- 1 STAR ANISE
- 1 LITRE OF FISH STOCK
- 4 X 25 ML PACKETS SQUID INK
- SALT AND PEPPER
- 500 G WASHED SPINACH
- 4 CANTABRIAN ANCHOVIES
- 20 SCALLOPS
- 1 LEMON

ALENA, RICARDO, BEN & PHIL

langans bistro

LANGANS BISTRO 26 DEVONSHIRE STREET LONDON W1 TEL 0207 935 4531

OPENING HOURS
MON-FRI 12.30-14.30 & 18.30-23.00,
SAT 18.30-23.00

CREDIT CARDS
VISA, MASTERCARD, AMEX, DINERS CLUB

In a city that offers just about every permutation of restaurant imaginable, it's always good to know of a consistent classic that you can rely on not to adopt a new look with every season. The bistro is all linen tablecloths, gleaming glassware and floor to ceiling eye candy. It transports you directly to vintage Paris and will feed you in much the same manner. Comforting, honest cuisine like Lamb hotpot or Trout with saffron rice and Pernod sauce. The dishes are not priced individually. Choose either two or three courses from the whole menu. Accompany them with a decent wine from the concise but well assembled wine list, and voila - you'll regret nothing.

braised knuckle of lamb with rosemary and garlic cassoulet

"IT IS A CLASSIC 'BISTRO' STYLE DISH. GOOD VALUE, UNFUSSY AND AN ENTIRE MEAL"

After soaking the beans overnight, boil in fresh water until they are 3/4 cooked (2-2 1/2 hours) then strain. Cut the bacon into squares and fry until the fat is released. Add the finely chopped onion, crushed garlic, tomatoes and herbs. Add the lamb and seal in the bacon fat until it's reached a nice brown colour. Pour in the stock and simmer for approximately 2 hours or until the lamb comes away from the bone. Top up the stock and season. Add the beans and breadcrumbs on top. Place in the oven on a medium heat (180°C) for 1 hour, or until most of the stock has absorbed and the breadcrumbs have formed a crust. Serve immediately.

SERVE WITH A TOMATO AND HERB SALAD
WINE SUGGESTION YOUNG RED WINE

MAIN COURSE
- 400 G WHITE HARICOT BEANS
- 100 G STREAKY BACON
- 4 x 450 G KNUCKLES OF LAMB
- 1 LITRE VEAL OR LAMB STOCK
- 2 SPRIGS OF FRESH ROSEMARY
- 2 CUPS BREADCRUMBS
- 1 ONION
- 4 CLOVES OF GARLIC
- 2 TOMATOES
- 2 BAYLEAVES
- SALT AND PEPPER

pineapple cheesecake

"STARTED AS AN EXPERIMENT AND EXCEEDED EVERYONE'S EXPECTATIONS"

Place a 22 cm x 5 cm cake ring on a 25 cm cake board. Crush the biscuits and mix with the melted butter. Spread evenly into the cake ring. Place in the fridge to firm up. Peel, core and cut the pineapple into chunks and cook with 125 g of the caster sugar and a little water until soft. Cool and purée in a processor. Soak the leaves of gelatine in cold water until soft, then melt with a little hot water. Cream together the eggs, remaining sugar and cream cheese. Mix the gelatine with the purée and quickly fold it into the cheese, followed by the half whipped cream. Pour the mixture into the cake ring and leave to set for 4-5 hours.

SERVE WITH RASPBERRY COULIS

DESSERT
SERVES 10
- 250 G DIGESTIVE BISCUITS
- 125 G BUTTER
- 1 MEDIUM PINEAPPLE
- 175 G CASTER SUGAR
- 2 TABLESPOONS WARM WATER
- BRONZE GELATINE (FOR DIRECTIONS, SEE SACHETS)
- LITTLE HOT WATER
- 2 MEDIUM EGG YOLKS
- 300 G SOFT FULL FAT CREAM CHEESE
- 160 ML DOUBLE CREAM

DUARTE & LOUIS

lola's

LOLA'S THE MALL 359 UPPER STREET LONDON N1 TEL 0207 359 1932

OPENING HOURS
MON-FRI 12.00-14.30 & 18.30-23.00,
SAT 12.00-15.00 & 18.30-23.00,
SUN 12.00-15.00 & 19.00-22.00

CREDIT CARDS
VISA, MASTERCARD, AMEX, DINERS CLUB

Occupying the whole top floor of a former Islington tram shed is the rather charming Lola's. By day it's skylights and big arched windows fill it with light; by night it assumes a cozy, romantic atmosphere. A live pianist every evening makes a pleasant change to the usual CD background, and whets the appetite for chef Gary Lee's globally influenced, modern British dishes. There are good value set menus every lunch and dinner, and a regularly changing a la carte that consistently offers original and seasonally driven dishes. Lola's manages to maintain a wonderfully refined ambience, without the pomp and circumstance that can so often smother a good meal.

pan roasted salmon, parsley salad and aioli

First make the aioli. Blend the yolks, chopped anchovy and crushed garlic for around 5 minutes. Add the oil in a thin stream. Boiling water can be added for a thinner consistency. Lightly season the salmon with salt, pepper and crushed fennel seeds. Heat a little butter and oil in a large frying pan. Fry the salmon over a high heat for around 3 minutes on each side. Meanwhile place the picked parsley into a bowl with the capers, grated zest of 1 lemon, finely chopped anchovy, finely diced onion, grated parmesan and some olive oil. Gently toss together ensuring a thorough mix. To serve, scatter a plate with parsley salad, place the salmon on top and garnish with aioli and a wedge of lemon.

lemon tart

To make the pastry, place the flour and sugar in a chilled boil. Rub in the butter until the mixture is crumbly. Stir in the eggs and add the salt. Work the mixture until it holds together. Wrap in cling film and chill. Whisk together the eggs and the juice of the lemons. Gradually whisk in the caster sugar. Stir in the double cream. Refrigerate and allow to settle. When required, skim any froth from the surface and add the lemon zest. Line a flan ring with the pastry (3-4 mm thick). Cover with foil and fill with baking beans. Bake blind in a pre-heated oven (190°C) for 10-15 minutes. Pour into a blind baked pastry case and cook at 120°C until set and slightly browned.

MAIN COURSE

- 3 LARGE EGG YOLKS
- 4 ANCHOVY FILLETS
- 4 CLOVES OF GARLIC
- 500 ML VEGETABLE OIL
- 200 G SALMON FILLET
- SALT AND PEPPER
- 2 TABLESPOONS FENNEL SEEDS
- BUTTER
- OLIVE OIL
- BUNCH PARSLEY
- 10 G FINE CAPERS
- 2 LEMON
- 2 FILLETS ANCHOVY
- 10 G RED ONION
- 10 G PARMESAN
- 1 LEMON

DESSERT

- 9 EGGS
- 5 LARGE LEMONS
- 375 G CASTER SUGAR
- 250 ML DOUBLE CREAM
- 350 G SOFT FLOUR
- 100 G CASTER SUGAR
- 2 SMALL EGGS
- DASH OF SALT

JÉRÔME & GARY

café maroush

CAFÉ MAROUSH 68 EDGWARE ROAD LONDON W2 TEL 0207 224 9339

OPENING HOURS
MON–SUN 12.00–01.00

CREDIT CARDS
VISA, MASTERCARD, AMEX, DINERS CLUB

Edgeware Road could be called 'Little Lebanon'. Middle eastern restaurants, specialist shops and cafes fill almost its entire length, and the Maroush group has the lion's share of the eateries. Café Maroush is its newest and perhaps funkiest face. Head chef at all six restaurants is Mr. Hussein Khreis. He must be able to spread himself pretty thinly, as you'll find the same quality and authenticity of cooking at each place. Café Maroush offers all the old favourites - hummus, tabbouleh, shawarma; as well as a good few more 'adventurous' dishes. 'Nikhaat salad', for example, is fresh brains. Or how about 'fresh raw lamb's liver'? Whatever you choose, it's guaranteed to be very fresh and very genuine. One tip - Just don't ask what exactly the 'lamb's prize' is.

stuffed courgettes, aubergines and vine leaves

Slice the courgettes and aubergines in two, lengthways. Remove the seeds and main pulp from the insides and wash thoroughly. In a mixing bowl put the mincemeat, rice, finely chopped garlic and mint and seasoning and mix together thoroughly. Stuff a generous quantity of the mincemeat mixture into the courgettes and aubergines. Wash the vine leaves, lay flat and place some of the stuffing at one end. Roll the leaves up to form small, tight 'cigars'. Place the butter ghee in a large pot over a medium heat. When melted, add the courgettes, aubergines and vine leaves, tomato puree and the water. Bring to the boil and simmer for around 1 1/2 hours. Serve hot.

SERVE WITH RICE

MAIN COURSE
SERVES 5

- 1 KG BABY COURGETTES
- 500 G BABY AUBERGINES
- 500 G LAMB MINCEMEAT
- 300 G PUDDING RICE
- 5 CLOVES OF GARLIC
- A FEW MINT LEAVES
- 1 TEASPOON SALT
- 1 TEASPOON CINNAMON
- 1 TEASPOON BLACK PEPPER
- 30 VINE LEAVES
- 100 G BUTTER GHEE
- 3 TABLESPOONS TOMATO PUREE
- 750 ML WATER

mohallabiyeh

In a large bowl mix the cornflour and the water together to form a smooth blend. Boil up the milk in a large saucepan, add the sugar and stir. Slowly add the cornflour/water mix, little by little, then the rose water and simmer for 5 minutes, stirring all the time. Allow to cool down before placing in the fridge. Serve cold in dessert bowls. Garnish with the crushed pistachios.

A. RADI, WADIH, JOANNA, KATERYNA & S. LILIYA

DESSERT
SERVES 5

- 4 TEASPOONS CORNFLOUR
- 100 ML WATER
- 1 LITRE MILK
- 200 G SUGAR
- 1 TABLESPOON ROSE WATER
- 100 G PISTACHIO NUTS

meson bilbao

MESON BILBAO 33 MALVERN ROAD LONDON NW6 TEL 0207 328 1744

OPENING HOURS
MON-THU 12.00-14.30 & 18.00-23.00,
FRI 12.00-14.30 & 19.00-23.30,
SAT 19.00-23.30

CREDIT CARDS
VISA, MASTERCARD

To say Jose Larrucea is passionate about cooking would be an understatement. "Basque cookery is the best in the world." He says, and whether you agree with him or not, it's difficult not to be impressed by his Basque cookery. This is Jose's first place after years spent working for others. The enthusiasm and devotion he feels for his native dishes really make a meal at Meson Bilbao special. As the food comes first, second and third on the agenda, the 'interior design' might have had to take a back seat. This is no bad thing, as the tatty football posters and plastic plants only add to the authenticity of the place. It is a perfect replica of a traditional Spanish tapas bar, right down to the decidedly lethal house Sangria.

hake koykera

In a large earthenware container add the hake, and
prawns along with the fish stock. Place in a pre-heated
oven at 160°C and cook until the prawns are almost
cooked, and the hake is coloured. Boil the eggs and
allow to cool. To the dish add the sliced onion, olive oil
and asparagus, potatoes (peeled and 3/4 boiled) and
clams. Season with salt and pepper. Return to the oven
and continue to cook until the clams have opened.
Remove from the oven, garnish with the eggs and
paprika and serve.

MAIN COURSE

- 750 G HAKE FILLETS
- 500 G KING PRAWNS
- 1 LITRE LIGHT FISH STOCK
- 4 EGGS
- 1 ONION
- OLIVE OIL
- 500 G GREEN ASPARAGUS
- 400 G POTATOES
- 2 TABLESPOONS PAPRIKA
- 500 G CLAMS
- SALT AND PEPPER

t-bone meson bilbao

Marinate the steaks in the olive oil, finely chopped
garlic and parsley for 2-3 hours (or overnight if
possible). Heat a griddle pan until smoking hot.
Meanwhile, cover the steaks thoroughly in
breadcrumbs and lay on the sizzling griddle. The
breadcrumbs act as a sealant and ensure the moisture
remains. Cook for 1-1 1/2 minutes either side. The
steaks should be served very rare.

SERVE WITH BOILED POTATOES
WINE SUGGESTION HEAVY RIOJA

MAIN COURSE

- 4 X MEDIUM T-BONE STEAKS
- OLIVE OIL
- 4 CLOVES OF GARLIC
- BUNCH PARSLEY
- 200 G BREADCRUMBS

DENNIS & PACO

mildred's

OPENING HOURS
MON-SAT 12.00-23.00

CREDIT CARDS
ARE NOT ACCEPTED

When Jane Muir and Diane Thomas opened Mildred's over a decade ago, they had in mind a real alternative to the rather purist notion of vegetarian eateries that had become synonymous with a meat free diet. They wanted to offer a place where veggies and carnivores alike could go and eat tasty food that just happened to be meat free. The philosophy worked, and it is still in place today. At both lunch and dinner times there are interesting globally influenced dishes on offer - the sort that you might want to try for their own sake, not just because they are vegetarian. Chef Jill Campbell stocks the menu from her own extensive list of recipes, which means a daily choice of dishes varied enough to temp just about everyone.

smoked cheese and rocket polenta with roasted root vegetables, garlic and red wine sauce

"IT'S A GOOD ALTERNATIVE TO SUNDAY LUNCH"

Firstly, roast the vegetables. Blanche the parsnips and fennel and drain. Place all the vegetables on a baking tray. Mix the sugar, oil, vinegar, salt and pepper together and pour over the vegetables. Roast in the centre of a 180°C oven, and roast until they are soft but still holding their shape. Next place all the ingredients for the red wine sauce into a large pot and simmer until the tomatoes have softened and the wine reduced. Blend well and pass through a sieve. Finally, in a large pot put 75 grams of the cubed butter, milk, mustard, salt, pepper and water and bring to a rapid simmer. Whisk in the polenta, stir for a couple of minutes and add the grated cheese, chopped rocket, and rest of the butter. Carry on stirring until smooth. Pour onto a flat tray and chill until needed. To serve, cut the polenta into 4 circles and grill until warm. Divide the vegetables and place on top of the polenta portions. Drizzle some of the red wine sauce over and serve.

WINE SUGGESTION A ROBUST RED WINE

- 2 PARSNIPS
- 1 FENNEL BULB
- 2 CARROTS
- 1 LARGE SWEET POTATO
- * 2 RED ONIONS
- 1 CELERIAC
- 12 HEAPED TABLESPOONS LIGHT MUSCOVADO SUGAR
- 300 ML OLIVE OIL
- 300 ML BALSAMIC VINEGAR
- SALT AND PEPPER
- 6 CLOVES OF GARLIC
- 700 G RIPE TOMATOES
- 500 ML RED WINE
- 2 HEAPED TABLESPOONS LIGHT MUSCOVADO • SUGAR
- 125 G BUTTER
- 100 G BUTTER
- 250 ML MILK
- 1 TABLESPOON DIJON MUSTARD
- SALT AND PEPPER
- 500 ML WATER
- 185 G INSTANT POLENTA
- 250 G SMOKED CHEESE
- 50 G WILD ROCKET

KATHY & MATTHEW

momo

OPENING HOURS
MON–FRI 12.30–14.15 & 19.00–23.15,
SAT 19.00–23.15, SUN 19.00–22.00

CREDIT CARDS
VISA, MASTERCARD, AMEX, DINERS CLUB

From the first day that Mourad Mazouz opened the doors at Momo, it's been pretty much rammed. Just about anyone who's anyone has dined or drank or partied within its clay-clad walls. All low tables, candle lanterns and cushions, it's like a Hollywood set from some Moorish epic. Mazouz's North African cuisine is first rate. This is a man who takes his food very seriously. Dedicated to using authentic ingredients from his homeland, his dishes are awash with the spices and fragrances of the region. The restaurant menu, as with the cookbook from which these recipes have come (published by Simon and Schuster, priced at £25.00) is long and varied, and everything you'll find, from the breads to the bowls, are the real deal.

lhem lahlou
"SWEET LAMB STEW"

In the upper part of a steamer, steam the prunes for 30 minutes, until swollen. Leave to cool and remove the stones. Roll the prunes in the toasted sesame seeds. Cut the meat into chunks. Melt the butter in a large casserole dish. Add the meat, salt and pepper and fry on a medium heat, stirring, for about 10 minutes until the meat is an even light brown colour. Sprinkle on the ground cinnamon and add the cinnamon sticks. Add the sugar little by little. Add the orange-blossom water and water to cover. Bring to the boil, then reduce the heat and simmer for 20 minutes.Peel, core and thinly slice the apples and add them to the dish, along with the prunes. Cook, uncovered, for another 20 minutes to allow the water to evaporate. Check the seasoning and serve immediately.

SERVE WITH POTATO GRATIN WITH FRESH CORIANDER

MAIN COURSE
- 32 PRUNES
- 50 G SESAME SEEDS
- 1 KG LEAN, BONELESS LAMB
- 100 G UNSALTED BUTTER
- 1 TEASPOON SALT
- 1/2 TEASPOON GROUND WHITE PEPPER
- 1 TEASPOON GROUND CINNAMON
- 2 CINNAMON STICKS
- 150 G BROWN CASTER SUGAR
- 100 G ORANGE-BLOSSOM WATER
- 300 ML WATER
- 2 APPLES

couscous seffa

Soak the raisins in the warm tea and leave to swell for an hour. Drain and keep aside. Steam the couscous. Add the sugar, orange-blossom water, three quarters of the cinnamon, salt, butter (cut into pieces) and the raisins to the couscous and mix thoroughly. Sprinkle with the remaining cinnamon and serve warm. Serve with the buttermilk, if using, in a carafe.

DESSERT
- 200 G WHITE SEEDLESS RAISINS
- 1 LITRE WARM TEA
- 500 G MEDIUM-GRADE COUSCOUS
- 80 G ICING SUGAR
- 100 ML ORANGE-BLOSSOM WATER
- 1/2 TEASPOON SALT
- 80 G UNSALTED BUTTER
- 1 TABLESPOON GROUND CINNAMON
- 1 LITRE BUTTERMILK (OPTIONAL)

JOHNSON, KAMEL, AURELIE & CELINE

nikitas

NIKITAS 65 IFIELD ROAD LONDON SW10 TEL 0207 352 6326

OPENING HOURS
TUE-SAT 19.00-23.30

Around thirty years ago on a largely residential Fulham street, a small outpost of Imperial Russia turned up. Nikitas has been there ever since. An institution, it was the very first of its kind in London. Made up by a series of low lit, interconnecting basement rooms, the place is a decadent riot. Purple, burgundy and blood red walls. Frescoed ceilings. Domes and arches everywhere. The concise menu offers trusty, classic Russianesque dishes and has probably remained pretty much unaltered since it was first put together by Chef Didi, way back when. However, with thirty different vodkas served by the shot or frozen carafe; it's not so much the food that pulls the crowds, as the… 'ambience'.

pirozhki

Pre-heat the oven to 180°C. Blend the finely chopped spinach, crumbled stilton and grated Parmesan together with a little oil until a creamy mixture forms. Season with salt and pepper. Roll out the puff pastry to around 5 mm thickness and cut into small, 2.5 cm diamonds. Put about a teaspoon of the cheese mixture onto each diamond. Brush all over with beaten egg yolk. Place in the oven for around 15 minutes, or until they are browned all over.

SERVE WITH PLUM VODKA

STARTER

• 500 G SPINACH
• 250 G STILTON
• 250 G PARMESAN
• SALT AND PEPPER
• 500 G PUFF PASTRY
• 1 EGG YOLK
• OIL

shashlyk po-karski

Mix together the oil, crushed garlic, bay leaves, rosemary and seasoning. Marinade the pork in this for around 24 hours. Combine the yoghurt and finely chopped cucumber, and keep refrigerated. Chop the onions and peppers to 2.5 cm squares. Cut the marinated pork into 2.5 cm cubes. Assemble on skewers, a cube of pork, pepper, then onion until the skewer is around 3/4 full. Ideally chargrill. If this is not possible, place under a hot grill for around 3-4 minutes each side. Serve on skewers, on the plate with a good spoonful of the yoghurt/cucumber dip

SERVE WITH BASMATI RICE AND PEPPER VODKA

MAIN COURSE

• 3 TABLESPOONS EXTRA VIRGIN OLIVE OIL
• 3 CLOVES OF GARLIC
• 4 BAYLEAVES
• GOOD SPRIG OF ROSEMARY
• SALT AND PEPPER
• 450 G TRIMMED LOIN OF PORK
• SMALL TUB MATURED NATURAL YOGHURT
• LARGE CUCUMBER
• 2 MEDIUM ONIONS
• 2 GREEN PEPPERS

quality chop house

THE QUALITY CHOP HOUSE 92-94 FARRINGDON ROAD LONDON EC1 TEL 0207 837 5093

OPENING HOURS
LUNCH: MON-FRI 12.00-15.00,
SUN 12.00-16.00,
DINNER: MON-SAT 18.30-23.30,
SUN 19.00-23.30

CREDIT CARDS
VISA, MASTERCARD

'Progressive working class caterer' proclaims the etched window outside this Farringdon institution, and although the client base might have changed somewhat, hardly anything else about the front or interior has since 1869. Stepping into the 'Quality chop house' is to step back in time. Owner and chef Charles Fontaine serves up traditional British food in wholly traditional surroundings. Seated in the wooden booth benches, surrounded by original wallpaper, tiles and fittings it's impossible not to be transported back to a bygone era. The recent expansion next door has resulted in the 'Quality fish house'. Jellied eels and smoked Mackerel now sit alongside such classics as Steak and kidney pie and Corned beef hash. All quality ingredients, cooked to a meticulous agenda - Venerable dishes in a Victorian setting.

bang bang chicken

"WE ARE SEEN AS A TRADITIONAL BRITISH RESTAURANT, HOWEVER NOT ALL OUR DISHES ARE THAT ORTHODOX"

Finely slice the chicken breast. Mix the peanut butter with the grated ginger, sweet chilli sauce and olive oil. Dress the chicken with the sauce and garnish with finely sliced spring onion, cucumber and lettuce, tossed in olive oil and the juice of the lime.

SERVE WITH CRUSTY BREAD
WINE SUGGESTION AUSTRALIAN RIESLING

STARTER

- 2 SMOKED CHICKEN BREASTS
- 200 G SMOOTH PEANUT BUTTER
- 10 G ROOT GINGER
- 20 G SWEET CHILLI SAUCE
- 20 G OLIVE OIL
- 4 SPRING ONIONS
- 1/4 CUCUMBER
- 1/2 LETTUCE
- 1/2 LIME

corned beef hash

"ONE OF MOST POPULAR DISHES. FILLING, SAVORY AND TASTY"

Boil the beef in a large pan of water for three hours. Then remove from water and leave to cool. Trim all the fat from the beef. Cut it up into 2 cm lengths. Peel the potatoes, boil for 15-20 minutes and cut into 2 cm cubes. Slice the onions and fry in butter until golden brown. Combine the beef, potato and onions, Worcestershire sauce and seasoning. Stir-fry in an ovenproof pan for a few minutes then transfer to the oven. Cook for 20 minutes at 220°C. Present with a fried egg on top.

SERVE WITH BUTTERED CABBAGE AND CARROTS/CROZES HERMITAGE

MAIN COURSE

- 1 KG SALT BEEF BRISKET
- 1 KG POTATOES
- 250 G ONIONS
- BUTTER
- WORCESTERSHIRE SAUCE
- SALT AND PEPPER
- 4 EGGS

SONIA & MASON

quo vadis

QUO VADIS 26-29 DEAN STREET LONDON W1 TEL 0207 437 9585

OPENING HOURS
MON-FRI 12.00-14.30 & 18.00-23.30,
SAT 18.00-23.30, SUN 18.00-22.30

CREDIT CARDS
VISA, MASTERCARD, AMEX, DINERS CLUB

A bit of a Soho institution, Quo Vadis most recently came to prominence when the squabblings of Co-owners Marco Pierre White and Damien Hurst went public. Hirst pulled out of the venture, taking his works with him, which White promptly replaced with his own strangely 'Hirst-like' artworks. That aside, unsurprisingly, the food here is extremely good. Serious French cuisine, with service and atmosphere to match. Chef Spencer Patrick produces complex, high brow dishes with prices to match. A typical dish might be tartare of salmon with cucumber and dill, or roast poulet noir forestière, Madeira roasting juices. The wine list makes for lengthy reading and is every bit a serious as the food. Enjoy a digestive upstairs in the dark, slick bar, surrounded by more of those strangely familiar artworks.

grilled sea scallops with crispy calamari, sauce nero

Sweat the chopped shallots and finely chopped garlic together, not allowing them to colour. Add the white wine and peppercorns. Allow this to reduce by half then add the stock. Reduce this by a third. Add the cream and allow to reduce until it reached a sauce consistency. Add the squid ink and cook slowly for 8-10 minutes. Season and pass through a fine sieve. Heat a little olive oil in a non-stick pan. Add the scallops (out of shell) and cook for around 1 1/2 minutes on each side. Have the oil in the deep fryer preheated. Deep-fry the squid until crisp and golden. Season both the scallops and the squid with salt and lemon juice. To plate - place 3 scallops in the centre of each plate about 1 cm apart. Pour a little sauce over and around the scallops and top in the middle with a baby squid. Serve immediately.

grilled salmon with ventreche ham, savoy cabbage, sauce lie de vin

To make the sauce : sweat the finely chopped shallots. Add the alcohol, then the stocks and reduce by half. Add the cream and star anise and whisk in the butter. Season with salt and pepper. Keep warm. Blanch the cabbage in boiling, salted water along with the smoked bacon rinds. Cook for 2 minutes, drain well, remove the rinds, add the butter. Season with salt and freshly grated pepper. Under a pre-heated grill, grill the salmon for around 1 1/2 minutes on each side. Remove the salmon and place the ham under the grill, cook it very lightly without colouring. To serve, place the cabbage in the centre of each plate. Put the salmon on top and the ham on top of the salmon. Pour the sauce around.

STARTER

- 5 SHALLOTS
- 1/4 HEAD GARLIC
- 500 ML WHITE WINE
- 1 TEASPOON WHITE PEPPERCORNS
- 500 ML CHICKEN STOCK
- 300 ML DOUBLE CREAM
- 50 G SQUID INK
- SALT AND PEPPER
- OLIVE OIL
- 12 MEDIUM SCALLOPS
- VEGETABLE OIL FOR DEEP-FRYING
- 3 WHOLE BABY SQUIDS
- 1 LEMON

MAIN COURSE

- 2 SHALLOTS
- 650 ML RED WINE
- 85 ML RUBY PORT
- 250 ML FISH STOCK
- 250 ML VEAL STOCK
- 50 ML DOUBLE CREAM
- 1 STAR ANISE
- 160 G UNSALTED BUTTER
- SALT AND PEPPER
- 1 GOOD SIZED HEART SAVOY CABBAGE
- 1-2 SMOKED BACON RINDS
- 40 G UNSALTED BUTTER
- SALT AND PEPPER
- 4 X 150 G FILLETS SALMON
- 8 SLICES OF VENTRECHE HAM

ERIC & CURTIS

rain

RAIN 303 PORTOBELLO ROAD LONDON W10 TEL 0208 968 2001

OPENING HOURS
LUNCH: TUE-FRI 12.30-14.30,
SAT & SUN 11.30-16.00,
DINNER: MON-SAT 19.00-23.00

CREDIT CARDS
VISA, MASTERCARD, AMEX, DINERS CLUB

Rain's interior is a cacophony of mosaic, glass, drapery and twisted metal. You could be anywhere in the East, which is fitting, as the food mirrors the same regional ambiguity. Owner and Chef Sameer Vaswani grew up in Hong Kong and spent much of his youth travelling various parts of Asia. These experiences have inspired him to create dishes of genuine originality and sophistication. He calls it 'New Asian cuisine'. Imagine combining elements of your favourite Indian, Chinese, Thai and Japanese dishes onto one plate, and you will have some idea of the sort of food you'll find here. He doesn't try and spread his net too wide, and by sticking exclusively to Asian influences has produced an original hybrid, and one I feel we'll see widely imitated.

seared scallops with a lemongrass and coconut cream sauce

In a saucepan heat up the coconut cream and bring to the boil to release the flavour and aroma. Turn down the heat and leave to simmer. Bruise the lemongrass stalks, tear the lime leaves and cut the chillies in half lengthways. Add these to the coconut cream and reduce by almost half. Once reduced, add the fish sauce to taste. This will bring all the flavours together. Strain and keep to one side. Cut the asparagus into 4 cm tips and blanche. Put to one side. In a wok heat up the peanut oil. When the oil is extremely hot, season the scallops and add them to the wok, cooking on both sides until golden. Place 3 scallops per plate, spoon over a little coconut sauce (warm) and garnish with asparagus tips.

SERVE WITH RICE OR BREAD
WINE SUGGESTION RICHARD HAMILTON CHARDONNAY, AUSTRALIA

salmon sashimi on spring onion blinis with wasabi crème fraîche and caviar

Combine the crème fraîche and the wasabi and mix well so as to dissolve the wasabi paste. Add a little salt to taste and put to one side. Trim the spring onion stalks and blanche in salted water. Remove from boiling water and place directly in ice-cold water. Puree the spring onions in a blender. Add the egg, flour and seasoning and mix to form a batter. In a pan heat 2 tablespoons of vegetable oil, and when very hot add a spoonful of the blini mixture. You are looking for a crisp outside and a soft, cooked inside. If the mixture is too dry add a little milk or egg. If too liquid, add a little more flour. Using a sharp knife, slice the salmon fillet into 1/2 cm slices. Place on a blini (which should be at room temperature), add 1/2 a teaspoon of the wasabi crème fraîche and finish with as much caviar as desired. Garnish with a sprig of dill.

SERVE WITH DOM PERIGNON CUVEE, '85

SAMEER & GUNDA

ransome's dock

RANSOME'S DOCK 35-37 PARKGATE ROAD LONDON SW11 TEL 0207 223 1611

OPENING HOURS
MON-FRI 11.30-23.00, SAT 11.30-24.00,
SUN 11.30-15.30

CREDIT CARDS
VISA, MASTERCARD, AMEX, DINERS CLUB

Although this is owner and head chef Martin Lam's first solo venture, he is no stranger to the London restaurant scene; head chef at Le Caprice and L'Escargot being just a couple of his credentials. Ransome's Dock sits in an enviable position right on the river, overlooking one its small canal estuaries. In such calming surroundings you can enjoy food that Martin describes as 'produce led modern European'. Seasonality is a big factor for both the food and wine, the latter earning the restaurant the 'Most exceptional wine list' accolade at the Carlton Restaurant awards 2000. With 300 listed bottles and the same amount off the list, this is unsurprisingly a Mecca for grape enthusiasts, and as well as a fantastic choice, you will also find some of the best bottle prices in any London restaurant.

pan fried scallops with beetroot and walnut oil

"THE ROASTED BEETROOT COMPLIMENTS THE GOLDEN SCALLOPS PERFECTLY, BOTH IN FLAVOUR AND COLOUR"

MAIN COURSE
SERVES 6

- 6 MEDIUM BEETROOTS
- OLIVE OIL
- ROCK SALT
- 2 TABLESPOONS WALNUT OIL
- 1 DESSERTSPOON AGED SHERRY VINEGAR
- BLACK PEPPER
- 10 G BUTTER
- 12 LARGE SCALLOPS
- 1 TABLESPOON CHIVES

Wash the beetroot. Roll them in olive oil and rock salt then place in an ovenproof dish, cover and bake at gas mark 4 (180°C) for 2 hours. Once cooked leave to reach room temperature then cut them into 5 mm slices. Dress them in walnut oil, vinegar, salt and pepper then leave for flavours to combine for around 20 minutes. Meanwhile slice the scallops in half horizontally. Melt equal parts of butter and olive oil in a heavy frying pan. When the pan is hot cook, firstly the scallop roe for 1 minute, then add the sliced white meat for 45 seconds each side. Season with salt and pepper and serve immediately, with the scallops on top of the sliced beetroot and a scattering of chopped chives.

WINE SUGGESTION MOSS WOOD SEMILLON FROM MARGARET RIVER, AUSTRALIA OR KUMEU RIVER CHARDONNAY, NEW ZEALAND

warm croustillant of figs with pinot noir sauce

Roll out the puff pastry and cut to approximately 11 cm diameter circles, keep chilled. Beat the eggs and 80 g caster sugar together to achieve a nice smooth consistency. Fold in the ground almonds and whisk for three minutes over a pan of boiling water. Remove from heat and stir in 2 teaspoons of the cognac or armagnac. Allow to cool. Spoon some of the mixture on to each pastry circle to about 1.5 cm thickness, leaving a 1 cm gap around the outside edge. Slice each fig into 6 equal wedges. Place 2 figs (12 slices) on a circle pattern on each pastry and bake in a hot oven for 15 minutes, until the pastry is cooked and a nice colour has been achieved. Meanwhile, boil up 1 bottle of good fruity Pinot Noir with 350 g sugar until it achieves a syrupy texture. Sprinkle each croustillant with caster sugar and flash under the grill. Serve with a good spoonful of the Pinot Noir sauce.

WINE SUGGESTION VEUVE CLICQUOT CHAMPAGNE

DESSERT
- 900 G BUTTER PUFF PASTRY
- 2 EGGS
- 450 G CASTER SUGAR
- 80 G GROUND ALMONDS
- COGNAC OR ARMAGNAC
- 8 RIPE FIGS
- 1 BOTTLE PINOT NOIR

MARTIN

rasa

RASA W1 6 DERING STREET LONDON W1 TEL 0207 629 1346

OPENING HOURS
MON-SAT 12.00-15.00 & 18.00-23.00,
SUN 18.00-23.00

CREDIT CARDS
VISA, MASTERCARD, AMEX, DINERS CLUB

Das Sreedharan swapped a promising life in accountancy for a rather racier life as a chef and restaurateur. In1994 he opened his first branch of Rasa, up in Stoke Newington, specializing in 'Kerala' vegetarian cooking. It was soon pulling the punters in from all over. Rasa W1 opened in 1998, and offers the same sort of food, in a slightly more upmarket location. Kerala is in the South of India, and Rasa's recipes are very typical of that region's 'home-style' cooking. Thus, a lot of fruits, nuts and delicate spicing. Dishes are never overpoweringly hot, and more often than not are accompanied by breads and pancakes (dosa's), rather than rice. Its plethora of awards and recommendations, including Time Out - 'Best vegetarian restaurant', twice, speak for themselves. Recipes are taken from Das's book 'Fresh flavours of India', published by Conran Octopus

cashew nut pakodas

Using a pestle and mortar, grind the finely chopped ginger and sliced chilli to a fine paste. Place in a large bowl with the cashews, rice flour, roughly chopped coriander, black sesame seeds, ghee and a little salt. Add 3 tablespoons of water and combine to form a slightly sticky mix. Take small amounts of the mixture and shape them into golfball-sized pieces. (Add a little more water if mixture is not holding together). Slightly flatten the balls. Heat some oil in a deep fryer, wok or large, heavy saucepan. Cook the pakodas, one at a time, in very hot oil for 5 minutes, turning once. When they are golden, drain on kitchen paper and serve.

SERVE WITH GARLIC PICKLE

STARTER

• 2.5 CM CUBE FRESH GINGER

• 1 GREEN CHILLI

• 300 G RAW CASHEW NUTS

• 200 G RICE FLOUR

• 2 TABLESPOONS CORIANDER LEAVES

• 1 TABLESPOON BLACK SESAME SEEDS

• 1 TABLESPOON GHEE

• 3 TABLESPOONS WATER

• VEGETABLE OIL FOR FRYING

• SALT

ripe banana pachadi

Using a spice mill, or pestle and mortar, grind together the freshly grated or desiccated coconut, sliced chillies and mustard seeds with 1 tablespoon of water to make a paste. Peel the plantain and cut it into 2.5 cm pieces. In a large saucepan, heat 3 tablespoons of the oil and stir fry the plantain for 5 minutes. Add a little salt to taste and 125 ml of water. Reduce the heat, mix in the spice paste and cook for 2 minutes. Add the yoghurt and cook, stirring constantly, for 5 minutes. In a small frying pan, heat the remaining 1 tablespoon of oil. Add the dried chillies and curry leaves, then pour the contents of the pan over the curry and gently stir through. Serve hot.

MAIN COURSE

• 50 G COCONUT

• 2 GREEN CHILLIES

• 1 TABLESPOON MUSTARD SEEDS

• 1 TABLESPOON WATER

• 450 G RIPE PLANTAIN

• 4 TABLESPOONS OIL

• 200 ML PLAIN YOGHURT

• 3 DRIED RED CHILLIES

• A FEW CURRY LEAVES

• SALT

SARJUN & CALISTO

the real greek

THE REAL GREEK 15 HOXTON MARKET LONDON N1 TEL 0207 739 8212

OPENING HOURS
MON-SAT 12.00-15.00 & 17.30-22.30

CREDIT CARDS
VISA, MASTERCARD

The blue painted exterior of 'The real Greek' is about the only thing that conforms to most clichés of that region. It's really out on a limb, as it must be the only eatery serving an alternative to the heavily Cypriot influenced 'Greek' cuisine on offer over here - hence the real Greek. Owner and head chef Theodore Kyriakou has split his homeland into six major categories, covering the whole geography of the region. He draws heavily on both historical and contemporary recipes, and given Greece's mixed history, that includes Italian and Middle Eastern as well as the Turkish influences. Winner of Time Out's best new comer award for 2000, and nominated in five of The Carlton restaurant award categories, rest assured that a meal here will consist of a whole lot more than Souvlaki and warm Retsina.

puree of aubergine

"FOR THIS DISH FOOD PROCESSORS ARE
BANNED! THE RIGHT TEXTURE IS ONLY ACHIEVED
BY HAND WITH A KNIFE"

Char the aubergine thoroughly over a gas ring, on a
barbecue or under the grill. When it is well coloured
(not blackened), chop it very finely with a knife. As you
are doing this add the finely chopped shallots, crushed
garlic, peeled, de-seeded and diced tomatoes and the
finely chopped parsley. Finally mix in the oil and
vinegar and seasoning.

roast chicken with yoghurt

"THIS IS A CRETAN FAVOURITE. ON THE FACE OF IT, IT LOOKS
A LITTLE STRANGE BUT PERSEVERE... IT'S WORTH IT"

Grate the lemon skins and save the zest, then squeeze
them and save the juice. Wash the outside of the
chicken with the lemon juice and rub the zest into the
cavity. Put the chicken in the fridge to marinade for 2-3
hours. Pre-heat the oven to 220°C. Place the chicken on
a roasting tray, season it well and pour the oil, butter
and 100 ml of water over it. Roast it for 20 minutes.
Turn the heat down to 180°C and roast for a further 50
minutes. Put the yoghurt, eggs and remaining water
into a mixing bowl and beat together. Pour the mix
over the chicken and return to the oven for a further 15
minutes, or until the sauce has thickened.

SERVE WITH PAN SCRAPINGS MAKE A DELICIOUS SAUCE
FOR THE CHICKEN. SERVE WITH A RICE PILAF
WINE SUGGESTION AMETHYSTOS RED, GREECE

STARTER

- 1 LARGE AUBERGINE
- 150 G SHALLOTS
- 2 CLOVES OF GARLIC
- 100 G FRESH PLUM TOMATOES
- 30 G FLAT PARSLEY
- 70 ML EXTRA VIRGIN OLIVE OIL
- 15 ML GREEK AGED WINE VINEGAR
- SALT AND BLACK PEPPER

MAIN COURSE

- 2 UN-WAXED LEMONS
- 1.5 KG CHICKEN
- SALT AND BLACK PEPPER
- 150 ML EXTRA VIRGIN OLIVE OIL
- 2 x 30 ML SPOONS BUTTER
- 170 ML WATER
- 500 ML GREEK YOGHURT
- 4 MEDIUM EGGS

PAULO, AL, EDDIE, AMANDA & CHARLY

royal china

OPENING HOURS
MON-SAT 12.00-23.00, SUN 11.00-22.00

CREDIT CARDS
VISA, MASTERCARD, AMEX, DINERS CLUB

One day, someone will slap a preservation order on the Royal China, and it will become a textbook example of how to decorate a traditional British-Chinese restaurant. Black lacquer covers just about every available space, heavily inlaid with golden bamboo shoots, dragons and lions. May it never change. The same can be said for the food. Nothing overly experimental or 'progressive', just perfectly executed classic Chinese dishes. Tangy sweet and sours, rich black and yellow bean sauces, fine noodles and the essential crispy ducks and barbequed pork. Royal China is also something of a master of those Moorish little parcels, Dim Sum, and there is always a healthy Oriental contingent tucking into the crispy chickens feet or cuttlefish dumplings every lunchtime - which says it all really.

steamed dim sum ribs

Crush the garlic and finely slice the chillies. Combine all the ingredients, bar the ribs. Thoroughly mix to form a paste. Separate the ribs and smear the mix all over them, ensuring all parts are covered. Leave to marinade for 2-3 hours, or preferably overnight in the fridge. In a steamer or a colander over a pan of boiling water, steam the ribs for around 7-10 minutes, or until the meat is thoroughly cooked.

SERVE WITH HOI SIN DIPPING SAUCE

STARTER

- 4 CLOVES OF GARLIC
- 1 WHOLE CHILLI PEPPER
- 20 G FLOUR
- 1 TEASPOON SALT
- 1 TEASPOON CHICKEN POWDER
- 1 TEASPOON SUGAR
- 1 TEASPOON SESAME OIL
- 2 TABLESPOONS PEANUT OIL
- 1 TEASPOON OF BLACK BEAN SAUCE
- 500 G SPARE RIBS OF PORK

stir-fry prawns with lemongrass

Heat a little oil in a wok or large frying pan. Firstly cook the cornflour and seafood stock for around 1 minute. Dice the onion, mango and peppers; crush the garlic. Combine these with the remaining ingredients, bar the prawns and cook on a medium heat for around 1 minute. Add the prawns and cook, stirring constantly so as to combine all the flavours. When the prawns turn pink, they are cooked. Serve immediately.

SERVE WITH EGG FRIED RICE

MAIN COURSE

- VEGETABLE OIL
- 2 TEASPOONS CORNFLOUR
- 2 TABLESPOONS SEAFOOD STOCK
- 1 SPRING ONION
- 1/2 A MANGO
- 1/2 SWEET RED PEPPER
- 1/2 SWEET GREEN PEPPER
- 1 CLOVE OF GARLIC
- 4 SLICES GINGER
- 1/2 TABLESPOON TOMATO KETCHUP
- 1/2 TEASPOON SALT
- 2 TEASPOONS SUGAR
- 1/2 TEASPOON CHICKEN STOCK POWDER
- 225 G MEDIUM SIZED KING PRAWNS

BOBO LET, LONG MAN

seven

SEVEN 1 LEICESTER SQUARE LONDON WC2 TEL 0207 909 1177

OPENING HOURS
MON-FRI 12.00-15.00, 18.00-24.00,
SAT 18.00-24.00

CREDIT CARDS
VISA, MASTERCARD, AMEX

Seven, in the heart of Leicester square, benefits from one of the best views in the city. It sits at the very top of Europe's largest nightclub - 'Home'. A glazed elevator whisks you up to the seventh floor and the spacious, elegant restaurant. Huge windows fill the outer wall, using London's skyline as a backdrop, with a narrow terrace running the length of it for vertiginous al fresco dining. Every aspect of Seven has been well thought through; the restrooms alone merit a visit; and the chic design is very much reflected in the food. Modern European dishes arrive well cooked and stylishly presented. And should you over indulge, worry not - a post dinner workout in the club is only a couple of floors away.

stuffed piquillos peppers with brandade and jabugo ham

Heat a spoon full of olive oil in a pan and roast the cod on top of the stove until it is golden brown. Flake and set it aside. Cook the peeled and diced potato in the milk with the garlic, salt and pepper. Drain well and puree with the remaining 3 tablespoons of olive oil. Using a spatula, add the flaked cod in with the potato, add the julienne ham and chopped parsley. Season to taste. Stuff each pepper with a little of the mixture, and warm through in a low oven until the are soft and cooked. Heat the chicken jus; add the tomato concasse, chopped parsley and oil. Serve the peppers with a little sauce over each.

grilled calf's liver, sage and onion mash, sauce diable

For the sauce: sweat the sliced shallots and the chrushed white peppercorns in oil. Add the caramelised chicken wings, vinegar, wine and reduce. Cover with chicken stock and cook for around 20 minutes. Once it has reduced, strain it and set aside. For the potatoes: peel and cut the potatoes into 5 cm dices and cook in seasoned, boiling water for around 10 minutes. Purée along with the shallot confit. Reduce the cream by half and work it into the potato with the butter and blanched sage. For the liver: Dust each slice in seasoned flour and griddle on a hot grill pan for around 1-2 minutes each side. Serve potato, topped by the liver with a splash of sauce.

STARTER
- 4 TABLESPOONS EXTRA VIRGIN OLIVE OIL
- 400 G SALTED AND DRIED COD FILLETS
- 300 G POTATO
- 500 ML MILK
- 2 CLOVES OF GARLIC
- SALT AND PEPPER
- 175 G JABUGO HAM
- 2 TEASPOONS FLAT LEAF PARSLEY
- 12 PIQUILLOS PEPPERS
- 200 ML CHICKEN JUS
- 200 G TOMATO CONCASSE
- 2 TEASPOONS FLAT LEAF PARSLEY
- 100 ML EXTRA VIRGIN OLIVE OIL

MAIN COURSE
- 2 SHALLOTS
- 20 G WHITE PEPPERCORNS
- OLIVE OIL
- 450 G CHICKEN WINGS
- 100 ML SHERRY VINEGAR
- 100 ML WHITE WINE
- 600 ML CHICKEN STOCK
- 800 G DESIREE POTATOES
- SALT AND FRESHLY GROUND WHITE PEPPER
- 50 G CONFIT SHALLOT
- 80 ML DOUBLE CREAM
- 180 G UNSALTED BUTTER
- JULIENNE OF SAGE
- 4 X 150 G SLICES CALF'S LIVER (1 CM THICK)
- PLAIN FLOUR

springbok café

THE SPRINGBOK CAFÉ 42 DEVONSHIRE ROAD LONDON W4 TEL 0208 742 3149

OPENING HOURS
MON-SAT 18.30-23.00

CREDIT CARDS
VISA, MASTERCARD

Springbok café can certainly claim to be London's only South African restaurant, and probably boast it's most exotic menu. 'Explore South Africa with a knife and fork' is it's motto, and they mean it. Zebra, Hottentot, Turtledove, and Blesbok are just a few of its regular offerings. This is perhaps not the best place to take an ardent vegetarian, but for carnivores it's an Aladdin's cave. Owner Pete Gottgens commitment to the wild and wonderful is thorough. He airfreights most of his stock in to ensure a regular supply of fresh quality produce. Side dishes and accompaniments are no less unusual. 'Morogo with shredded peppadews' for example or 'sauté madumbis and purple potatoes'. Eccentric eating to say the least.

bobotie salad

Sauté the finely chopped onion. Add the ginger, turmeric, jam, masala and chutney. Cook for one minute. Add the mince and mix thoroughly. Cook for 15 minutes. Add seasoning. Drain the mince to remove any excess fat. Whisk 2 eggs. Pack a round or oval dish with the mince mixture (bobotie) and pour the egg over the top. Place under a medium grill until the egg is cooked and golden. Dress the rocket in olive oil, salt and pepper. Place the leaves in the middle of the plate. Sprinkle the diced pepper around. Carefully remove the bobotie from mould and place on top.

pan fried springbok fillet with butternut, red pepper and leeks

Brown the veal bones and vegetables. Add water to cover in a stockpot. Simmer overnight. Strain the stock, retaining the liquid. Add tomato paste, wine and sugar to the stock and reduce to a desired consistency. Season. Pan fry the springbok (rare). Fry the sliced leek, sliced red pepper and cubed and blanched butternut in a little olive oil. Then compress them in a round ring mould to about 1/4 from the top. Slice the springbok and arrange on top of the vegetables in the mould. Carefully place the ring on a plate and remove the mould. Garnish with chives and dahnia. Drizzle some demi-glace around the plate.

STARTER

- 1 SMALL ONION
- 10 ML GINGER
- 15 ML TURMERIC
- 30 ML APRICOT JAM
- 20 ML MASALA PASTE
- 50 ML CHUTNEY
- 500 G MINCED LAMB
- SALT AND PEPPER
- 2 EGGS
- ROCKET LEAVES
- OLIVE OIL
- SALT AND PEPPER
- 60 ML RED PEPPER

MAIN COURSE

- 5 KG VEAL BONES
- 6 CARROTS
- 1 BUNCH CELERY
- 3 LEEKS
- 6 ONIONS
- WATER
- 150 ML TOMATO PASTE
- 2 LITRE RED WINE
- 200 ML DEMERERA SUGAR
- SALT AND PEPPER
- 4 X 180 G SPRINGBOK FILLETS
- 1 LEEK
- 80 G RED PEPPER
- 240 G BUTTERNUT
- OLIVE OIL
- 20 G CHIVES
- DAHNIA

PETE

st. john

ST. JOHN 26 SAINT JOHN STREET LONDON EC1 TEL 0207 251 0848

OPENING HOURS
MON-FRI 12.00-15.00 & 18.00-23.00,
SAT 18.00-23.00

CREDIT CARDS
VISA, MASTERCARD, AMEX, DINERS CLUB

Fergus Henderson coined the term 'Nose to tail eating' to define his approach to cooking, and he really means it. A model of resourcefulness, not a morsel is left un-used. Being a dedicated carnivore, his book - 'Nose to tale eating - a kind of British cooking' (Published by Macmillan), has a use for every part of an animals anatomy, from brains to brawn.

St. John is probably the most British of British restaurants. Wonderful, half forgotten recipes find themselves centre stage amongst a good few of Fergus' more inventive dishes. Its stark décor is reflected on the plates too. No pointless garnishes or superfluous ingredients. Just passionately cooked, honestly presented tucker from a man who's not afraid to call a spleen a spleen.

mussels, cucumber and dill

In a lidded pan, large enough to fit the mussels, heat up a splash of oil and gently fry the chopped onion and celery for a couple of minutes. Do not let them brown. Season heartily then add the tied bunch of thyme, mussels and wine. Stir to combine the ingredients and cover. Cook the mussels, shaking the pan now and then. When the mussels open, they are cooked. Remove from the heat and allow to cool. Once they have cooled, pluck the mussels from their shells, strain and reserve the liquor. To make the salad, cut the cucumber into 6 cm lengths, then split in half, then cut into three lengthways, aiming the blade at the centre of cucumber. Slice the onion thinly. Combine all the other ingredients and serve immediately.

roast bone marrow with parsley salad

Put the marrowbone in an ovenproof frying pan and place in a hot oven. Cook for around 20 minutes, though this may vary depending on the thickness of the bones. You are looking for the marrow to be loose and giving, but not melted away. Meanwhile lightly chop the parsley, mix it with the finely sliced shallots and capers, and at the last moment dress with oil, lemon, a pinch of salt and pepper. Serve with piles of toast. To eat, scrape the marrow onto the toast, season with coarse sea salt and top with a little of the salad.

STARTER
- OLIVE OIL
- 2 ONIONS
- 2 STICKS OF CELERY
- SALT AND PEPPER
- 1/2 BUNCH THYME
- 2 KG MUSSELS
- 1/4 BOTTLE DRY WHITE WINE
- 1 CUCUMBER
- 1 RED ONION
- HANDFUL OF EXTRA-FINE CAPERS
- BUNCH DILL
- JUICE OF 1 LEMON

MAIN COURSE
- 12 X 7-8 PIECES MIDDLE VEAL MARROWBONE
- A HEALTHY BUNCH FLAT PARSLEY
- 2 SHALLOTS
- 1 MODEST HANDFUL EXTRA-FINE CAPERS
- EXTRA VIRGIN OLIVE OIL
- JUICE OF 1 LEMON
- SEA SALT AND PEPPER
- GOOD SUPPLY OF TOAST

JUSTIN, JOHN, FERGUS, THOMAS & NEIL

sugar club

THE SUGAR CLUB 21 WARWICK STREET LONDON W1 TEL 0207 437 7776

OPENING HOURS
MON-SUN 12.00-15.00 & 18.00-23.00

CREDIT CARDS
VISA, MASTERCARD, AMEX, DINERS CLUB

In its first incarnation over in Notting Hill, The Sugar Club was like a closely guarded secret. Locals jealously filled the place as if it were their own private dining room. Now the original site has morphed into sibling Bali Sugar and the Sugar Club has moved to larger premises in the West End, leaving everyone happy. Global fusion is the easiest definition of antipodean chef David Selex's menus. A largely pacific base of ingredients is merged with any item that he might find interesting. If this approach to cooking might seem a little gung-ho, the results are anything but. Strong, contrasting original flavours. Precisely cooked and stylishly presented food, make for the kind of eating that inspired such fervent loyalty from day one.

shiitake mushroom broth with soba noodles, tofu and prawns

Place water, celery, onion, dried shitake, kombu, carrot and leek in a large pan. Simmer for 40 minutes until liquid is nicely flavoured. Drain liquid into a second pan, season with salt and a couple of dashes of light soy. Boil the noodles and divide into 4 bowls. Drop the fresh, finely sliced shitake, peeled prawns, tofu (diced into 1 cm blocks) and sliced spring onion into the hot broth, until prawns are cooked. Divide the broth between the 4 bowls. Finish with a few drops of sesame oil.

SERVE WITH ICE COLD BEER

STARTER

- 2 LITRES OF WATER
- 2 CELERY STALKS
- 1 WHITE ONION
- 15 DRIED SHIITAKE
- 1 SMALL PIECE KOMBU
- 1/2 CARROT
- 1 SMALL LEEK
- SALT
- LIGHT SOY
- 1 PACKET SOBA NOODLES
- 1 BUNCH SPRING ONION
- 6 FRESH SHITAKE
- 16 LARGE FRESH PRAWNS
- 250 G TOFU
- SESAME OIL

lemongrass roast plums with mascarpone and lime

Pre-heat the oven to 200°C. Place stoned and halved plums into an oven tray. Add sugar, smashed lemongrass and vanilla pod (split and scraped). Roast until slightly softened. Remove from oven and leave to cool. The plums should look soft and glazed with the lemongrass/vanilla syrup. Scoop the plums onto plates and serve with a large ball of mascarpone on each and a wedge of lime.

SERVE WITH BISCOTTI OR SHORT BREAD
WINE SUGGESTION VIN SANTO

DESSERT

- 8 PLUMS
- 1/2 CUP SUGAR
- 3 STALKS LEMONGRASS
- 1 VANILLA POD
- 200 G MASCARPONE
- 1 LIME

GREG, JOSEPH & SHAMINA

teatro

TEATRO 93-107 SHAFTESBURY AVENUE LONDON W1 TEL 0207 494 3040

OPENING HOURS
MON-FRI 12.00-15.00 & 18.00-22.45,
SAT 18.00-22.45

CREDIT CARDS
VISA, MASTERCARD, AMEX, DINERS CLUB

Teatro, as you might expect, sits the heart of theatre land. A series of staircases and tapering corridors transport you from the crush of Shaftesbury Avenue, to the serene calm of its rather dapper dining room. Co-owned by actress Leslie Ash and ex-footballer Lee Chapman, this is a long way from certain other celebrity owned restaurants. The design of the whole space, from the foyer to the forks has been carefully considered, and the result is a modern, stylish restaurant, where you can eat very well at surprisingly affable prices. Stuart Gillie's loosely French menu covers many bases, with a number of particularly original and involved dishes. Both bars serve up a decent martini, although one is the Members bar, and if your names not down...

peppered tuna carpaccio

Prepare the tuna, cut off any fat or sinew and the bloodline. Grate the lemons and roll the tuna in the sea salt and zest. Roll the tuna in cling film and tie as tightly as possible. Marinate this for 12 hours. Wash off the tuna and roll in the crushed black peppercorns. Again roll in cling film, tying as tightly as possible. Freeze until the fish is hard enough to slice on a slicing machine. For the garnish, cut the celery, apple and cucumber into fine strips and cover with equal amounts of rice wine vinegar and grapeseed oil. Once the tuna is hard, slice it in approximately 1/4 cm strips, and arrange it directly onto the plate. Cover with the garnish and a few of the washed leaves.

STARTER

• 500 G BLUE FIN TUNA

• 2 LEMONS

• SEA SALT

• BLACK PEPPERCORNS

• 3 CELERY STICKS

• 1 GRANNY SMITH

• 1/2 CUCUMBER

• RICE WINE VINEGAR

• GRAPESEED OIL

• CORIANDER LEAVES

• CELERY LEAVES

braised shoulder of lamb

Season the shoulder of lamb and seal it in a little oil in a red-hot casserole dish. Once it has reached a light brown colour, remove it and add to the pan the garlic, onions, celery and leeks cut into large chunks. After sweating them for approximately 5 minutes, add the herbs and tomatoes. Return the lamb and add the white wine and enough water to just cover it. Bring to the boil. Add the ceps and saffron. Cover with a lid. Slowly braise in a low oven (130°C) for 6-7 hours. When the shoulder is cooked, remove all the bones. They should just fall away. Discard the vegetables, but keep the cepes to garnish the dish. Reduce the remaining stock to make a sauce.

SERVE WITH FONDANT POTATO

MAIN COURSE

• 1 SHOULDER OF LAMB

• OIL

• 3 CLOVES OF GARLIC

• 3 ONIONS

• 1 CELERY

• 3 LEEKS

• A FEW SPRIGS THYME

• A FEW ROSEMARY LEAVES

• A FEW SAGE LEAVES

• A FEW SPRIGS PARSLEY

• A FEW BASIL LEAVES

• 10 PLUM TOMATOES

• 250 ML WHITE WINE

• WATER

• 500 G FROZEN CEPS

• 1/2 G SAFFRON

STUART

the vale

THE VALE 99 CHIPPENHAM ROAD LONDON W9 TEL 0207 266 0990

OPENING HOURS
MON 19.00-23.30,
TUE-SAT 12.30-15.00 & 19.00-23.30,
SUN 12.30-15.00 & 19.00-22.30

CREDIT CARDS
VISA, MASTERCARD, DINERS CLUB

After all most as many face-lifts as Zsa Zsa Gabor, the Vale seems to have finally found a formula that works. Through the vision of co-owners Francesca Melman and Robin Tarver, the place was transformed back in '99, into a stylish and top-notch neighbourhood restaurant. Robin had worked in the kitchens of The Chiswick and The Square before branching out, and his daily changing menu displays the assurance and quality you would expect from such tutelage. Expect dishes like Char-grilled calves liver with polenta or Mussel, leek and saffron risotto, served in relaxed but attentive surroundings. And expect the place to be in the same hands for longer than a fortnight.

roast breast of wood pigeon
with truffled jerusalem artichoke puree and madeira sauce

First remove the breasts from the wood pigeons and chop the bones. Then make the Madeira sauce. In a heavy bottomed pan, brown the bones in oil over a high heat for 5 minutes. Add the chopped vegetables and garlic for a further 5 minutes. Add the Madeira, reduce the heat and simmer until it has reduced to a syrup. Add the thyme, chicken stock and water, simmer for around 1 hour, to form a light gravy. Peel the artichokes and place directly in a bowl of water with the lemon juice. Heat a little butter in a saucepan and add the drained artichokes. Lightly season and sweat, covered for around 10 minutes. When they are soft right through, purée in a processor with the double cream and a little truffle oil. Pan-fry the pigeon breasts in a hot pan for around 3 minutes each side. Set aside and leave to rest for a few minutes. Cut each breast into three slices, on an angle. Place them on top of a good spoonful of artichoke and spoon some Madeira around the edge.

WINE SUGGESTION NEW WORLD PINOT NOIR

MAIN COURSE

- 2 WHOLE WOOD PIGEONS
- 1 CARROT
- 1 CELERY STICK
- 1/2 ONION
- 5 WHOLE CLOVES OF GARLIC
- 1/2 BOTTLE MADEIRA
- BUNCH OF THYME
- 500 ML CHICKEN STOCK
- 500 ML WATER
- 500 G JERUSALEM ARTICHOKES
- 1 LEMON
- BUTTER
- SALT AND PEPPER
- 50 ML DOUBLE CREAM
- GOOD QUALITY WHITE TRUFFLE OIL

blood orange and passion fruit jelly

In a large saucepan, bring the passion fruit juice up to a simmer. Add the sugar and stir to dissolve. Remove from the heat. Soak the gelatine in cold water for a few minutes. Squeeze out any excess water and add to the juice. Leave to cool down to room temperature. Cut the blood oranges into segments and pat them dry. Divide the segments between 6 ramekins. Pour over the passion fruit jelly and leave to set in the fridge.

SERVE WITH CLOTTED CREAM ICE CREAM
WINE SUGGESTION ROSE CHAMPAGNE

DESSERT
SERVES 6

- 500 ML PASSION FRUIT JUICE
- 250 G CASTER SUGAR
- 4 LEAVES OF GELATINE
- 9 BLOOD ORANGES

FRANCESCA & DAVE

veeraswami

OPENING HOURS
MON–SAT 12.00-14.30 & 17.30-23.30,
SUN 12.30-15.00 & 18.00-22.00

CREDIT CARDS
VISA, MASTERCARD, AMEX, DINERS CLUB

Veeraswami opened in 1927 as England's very first Indian restaurant. The site was taken over in 1997 and totally transformed. It is now one of a small breed of new pioneers, dedicated to showing us a truly authentic version of the nation's favourite dish. The kitchen is manned by a number of chefs from all over the Indian continent who present genuine, regional cooking, as we would taste it in its native state. Recipes are sourced from palaces to street stalls, and scrupulous care is taken in both their preparation and presentation. India's rich and diverse past and present is represented here by a plethora of dishes, making a meal here as much a lesson in history as it is in cuisine. Certainly not your 8 pints and a vindaloo kind of place.

egg and chutney patties

Grind the chutney ingredients together in a blender.
Add 2-3 tablespoons of water if needed. Divide the mix
into 6 equal parts and place onto each, half a boiled
egg face down. Boil the potatoes and mash them.
Season. Divide the mashed potato and make six
patties with a dip in the middle. Place a chutney/egg
parcel into the dip and encase it in the potato. Mix the
whisked eggs and flour to form a batter. Dip each
patty into the batter and fry in very hot oil until they
are golden brown. Serve immediately.

- 1 1/2 CUPS CORIANDER LEAVES
- 1/2 COCONUT
- 2 CLOVES OF GARLIC
- 1 TEASPOON SUGAR
- JUICE OF 1/2 LEMON
- PINCH OF SALT
- 3 EGGS
- 500 G POTATOES
- 2 EGGS
- 1/2 CUP OF FLOUR
- 3 CUPS OF OIL

prawns with spring onions

Marinate the prawns in half of the turmeric, lemon
juice, salt and half of the chilli powder for around
1 hour. Heat the oil in a pan and cook the onions until
they are transparent. Add the ginger-garlic paste,
the remaining turmeric, chilli powder and a little salt.
Cook for a further 2 minutes. Add the fresh methi and
kasuri methi, coriander, green chilli and Kashmiri red
chilli, cooking for 4-5 minutes. Add 1 cup of water and
simmer. Pan fry the prawns and when they are almost
cooked, add the sauce to finish.

SERVE WITH RICE OR ROTI

MAIN COURSE

- 1 KG PRAWNS
- 1 TEASPOON TURMERIC
- 1 TABLESPOON LEMON JUICE
- 1 1/2 TEASPOONS SALT
- 1 1/2 TEASPOONS RED
  CHILLI POWDER
- 3/4 CUP OIL
- 20 BULBS SPRING ONION
- 4 TABLESPOONS GINGER-GARLIC PASTE
- 2 CUPS FRESH METHI
- 1 TEASPOON KASURI METHI
- 2 TABLESPOONS FRESH CORIANDER
- 1 TEASPOON GREEN CHILLI
- 2 TEASPOONS KASHMIRI RED CHILLI
- 1 CUP WATER

NAMITA & RANJIT

villandry foodstore

VILLANDRY FOODSTORE 170 GT. PORTLAND STREET LONDON W1 TEL 0207 631 3131

OPENING HOURS
MON-SUN 08.30-22.00

CREDIT CARDS
VISA, MASTERCARD, AMEX, DINERS CLUB

For anyone who's serious about food, Villandry Foodstore is quite simply the Garden of Eden. An absolute treasure trove of a foodstore is the centrepiece, to which the restaurant and separate bar/brasserie are attached, and supplied by. Just about every ingredient you could think of is available. Fine cured meats, fish, fresh fruits and vegetables, cheeses, breads - jars of this, bags of that. Owner Martha Greene is committed to supplying everything that a dedicated gourmet would need. With such a fine larder, it's no wonder that the restaurant dishes up ultra-fresh, wonderfully inspiring cuisine. Chef Steve Evenett-Watts changes the menu daily, according to what's new or caught his eye that morning. 'Please allow time as all our food is cooked to order' proclaims the menu header; and believe - it's well worth the wait.

flat bread

Melt the butter. Combine together with the other ingredients in a bowl, gently mixing until a soft ball of dough is formed. Wrap the dough in cling film and leave it to chill in the fridge for 30 minutes. When it is cool, break off ping-pong sized balls and roll each into a disc the thickness of a matchstick. Bake these discs in a hot oven (185°C) for 1-2 minutes until they are pale gold and slightly puffy.

SERVE WITH VARIOUS FILLINGS OF YOUR CHOICE

STARTER

- 50 ML BUTTER
- 500 G PLAIN FLOUR
- 250 ML TEPID WATER
- 1 CLOVE OF GARLIC
- 1 TEASPOON FENNEL SEEDS
- PINCH OF SALT
- PEPPER

sea bass with gremolata, puy lentils, spinach and crème fraîche

Pre-heat the oven to 180°C. For the gremolata mix the finely grated zest of the lemon, the finely chopped parsley and the finely chopped garlic. Set aside. Next wash and drain the puy lentils. Put them together with the cloves of garlic, carrot, celery and onion in a pan and cover with water. Bring to the boil and simmer until cooked (about 20-30 minutes). Drain and season with Maldon sea salt and coarsely ground black pepper. Keep warm. Heat an ovenproof pan with a dribble of olive oil until it is almost smoking. Season the bass fillets with salt and pepper and fry them skin side down for 30-40 seconds. Transfer the pan with the fillets to a heated oven (180°C) for around 6 minutes, or until the bass is cooked. Meanwhile, put the lentils in a large pan, together with the crème fraîche and gently bring it to a simmer. Add the spinach (stalks removed) and cook until it wilts. The mixture should look quite creamy. If it looks too wet, cook for a bit longer, until the liquid has evaporated slightly. If it is too dry, add a little more crème fraîche. Check the seasoning and divide the lentil/spinach mixture onto 4 plates. Place the bass fillets on top and sprinkle with the gremolata.

MAIN COURSE

- 1 LEMON
- 1 SMALL BUNCH FLAT LEAF PARSLEY
- 1-2 CLOVES OF GARLIC
- 225 G PUY LENTILS
- 2-3 CLOVES OF GARLIC
- 1 CARROT
- 1 PIECE CELERY STALK
- 1 SMALL ONION
- 3/4 PINT OF WATER
- MALDON SEA SALT
- PEPPER
- OLIVE OIL
- 4 X 175 G BASS FILLETS (COD CAN BE SUBSTITUTED)
- 1 SMALL CARTON CRÈME FRAÎCHE
- 1.5-2 KG FRESH SPINACH

wiz

OPENING HOURS

LUNCH: MON-FRI 12.00-15.30,
SAT & SUN 11.30-16.00,
DINNER: MON-WED 18.30-23.00,
THU-SAT 18.30-24.00

CREDIT CARDS

VISA, MASTERCARD, AMEX

'Wiz' is the latest set-up from partners Dave Wilby and TV uber-chef Antony Worralthomson. They describe the cuisine as international tapas, and as with their previous outlets, recipes rely heavily on local, seasonal and wherever possible organic produce. The concept of taking a traditionally Spanish idea on a world tour, takes a little getting used to but, unsurprisingly, in such capable hands it works very well. The beauty of 'Wiz' is that you can eat as little or as much as you feel, and that sampling a hearty chunk of the menu won't break the bank. Upstairs they have revamped another good idea - 'Woz'. Here they offer a set, five course banquet, for a reasonable sum, and encourage groups. Which is a good thing, as unashamed gluttony is never as much fun on your own.

mini salmon and smoked haddock fish cakes

Cook the haddock in enough milk to just cover it, along with some finely diced onion and carrot, bayleaf, peppercorns and 2 cloves until firm and just cooked. Remove from milk, allow to cool, then flake. Discard any skin and bones. Sweat the other onion, finely diced, in butter. Combine with the haddock, dry mashed potato, melted butter and anchovy essence in a mixer with a 'dough hook' attachment. Briefly steam the salmon. Into the haddock/potato mixture, fold in by hand the salmon, the chopped eggs, parsley and dill. Season to taste. If the mixture seems too dry at this point, add some of the poaching milk. Divide the mixture into 8 amounts and shape into patties. Dip each one firstly into the flour, then the egg and finally the breadcrumbs. Refrigerate for 2 hours before use. Pan fry in butter for around 5 minutes each side, until crisp and golden.

SERVE WITH SORREL HOLLANDAISE
WINE SUGGESTION WHITE SAUVIGNON
FROM NEW ZEALAND

STARTER
- 275 G SMOKED, UN-DYED HADDOCK FILLETS
- 175 G SALMON
- MILK
- 2 ONIONS
- 1 CARROT
- 1 BAYLEAF
- PEPPERCORNS
- 2 CLOVES
- 275 G POTATOES
- 50 G BUTTER
- 2 TEASPOONS ANCHOVY ESSENCE
- 2 HARD BOILED EGGS
- 2 TABLESPOONS CHOPPED PARSLEY
- 1 TABLESPOON CHOPPED DILL
- SALT AND PEPPER
- FLOUR FOR COATING
- BEATEN EGG FOR DIPPING
- NATURAL BREADCRUMBS
- 50 G BUTTER FOR FRYING

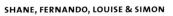

SHANE, FERNANDO, LOUISE & SIMON

zilli fish

OPENING HOURS
MON-SAT 12.00-23.30

CREDIT CARDS
VISA, MASTERCARD, AMEX, DINERS CLUB

Part of a number of Soho bastions owned by the very Italian Mr. Aldo Zilli. Zilli Fish is crowded, bustly and the service prompt and to the point. It's proximity makes it a regular favourite of Soho's media / music crowd, and their very busy mobile phones. Extremely good fish with fine Italian cookery makes for a pretty irresistible combination, as dishes like Monkfish wrapped in speck, or 'our famous' spaghetti lobster more than demonstrate. The menu always lists a number of interesting meat or vegetarian options. But fish is the real draw. Packs them in like sardines.

skewers of scallops with rosemary sprigs

"USE LARGE SCALLOPS, IF USING SMALLER, DOUBLE THE QUANTITY"

Pierce each scallop onto a rosemary sprig. Mix the lemon juice and 45 ml of olive oil and season with some sea salt. Marinate the scallops in the lemon for 10 minutes. Meanwhile, place the flour in a bowl and season with salt and pepper. Add the thinly sliced onion rings and coat all over. Heat the vegetable oil in a deep pan. When very hot, fry the onion rings in batches for 2-3 minutes or until crisp and golden. Drain on kitchen towel. Pre-heat the grill to medium hot. Place the scallops on a foil lined grill pan and cook for 4 minutes on each side, or until golden brown and tender. Arrange the scallops on large plates with a portion of onion rings. Drizzle with olive oil and sprinkle with the remaining salt flakes.

whole sea bass in salt and pepper crust

"A PORTUGUESE CLASSIC, IDEAL FOR DINNER PARTIES
AS IT'S SO SIMPLE"

Pre-heat the oven to 200°C. Mix together the sea salt, peppercorns and egg whites. Spread a little of the salt crust mixture on a large baking tray. Pat the gutted and gilled (not de-scaled) fish dry all over and place on top of the mixture on the tray. Press the remaining crust all over to enclose the fish completely. Roast for 20-25 minutes. Meanwhile, mix the remaining oil, lemon juice and black pepper in a small bowl. Heat a heavy-based frying pan until very hot and cook the two lemons, sliced thickly, for 2-3 minutes, until browned on both sides. Remove the fish from the oven and break open the crust. Peel away any remaining skin. Open out half the fish and remove the bones. Serve on a platter with the lemon dressing, parsley and lemon slices so everyone can help themselves and dress their own portions.

STARTER

- 8 KING SCALLOPS
- 8 LONG FRESH SPRIGS ROSEMARY
- 1 LEMON
- 75 ML EXTRA VIRGIN OLIVE OIL
- 15 ML SEA SALT FLAKES
- 50 G PLAIN FLOUR
- SALT
- VBLACK PEPPER
- 1 MEDIUM ONION
- VEGETABLE OIL

MAIN COURSE
SERVES 6

- 900 G COARSE SEA SALT
- 170 G MIXED PEPPERCORNS
- 2 EGG WHITES
- 2 KG FRESH SEA BASS
- 175 ML EXTRA VIRGIN OLIVE OIL
- 600 ML LEMON JUICE
- BLACK PEPPER
- 2 LEMONS
- 6 TABLESPOONS ROUGHLY CHOPPED FLAT-LEAF PARSLEY

addresses • alphabetical index • glossary • addre

glossary

À LA MINUTE dished that have to be served straight after cooking.

AL DENTE slightly undercooked so still firm.

AU BAIN MARIE to heat in a double boiler. You can also use a large pan, filled with warm water in which you place a smaller pan or bowl.

BLANCH to cook cleaned vegetables briefly in boiling water. After boiling rinse directly with cold water to stop the cooking process.

BOUQUET GARNI small bunch of parsley, thyme, laurel, leek and other herbs. Tied together and added to soup or for poaching fish. To be removed after cooking.

BRAISE to cook vegetables and meat cooked in butter, oil or lard with the lid on the pan.

BRINE solution of water and salt (30 gr. salt to a litre). Used to preserve meat, fish and vegetables.

CARVE to carve into slices.

CLARIFY clarified butter is made by heating butter slowly and taking out the white part.

COMPOTE sauce made with fresh or tinned fruits, cooked with sugar. Served as an accompaniment to game and poultry.

COURT-BOUILLON vegetable stock used to poach fish.

DRESS to finish a dish by arranging artfully on a plate.

DUXELLE finely chopped mushrooms, shallots and herbs stewed in butter.

FARCE a mixture of finely chopped ingredients used for stuffing, game, poultry or meat.

FERMENT soy sauce is a fermented product.

FILLET to cut away the bones from fish or meat.

FLAMBÉ to sprinkle a dish with alcohol and set on fire.

FOND reduced stock made from the bones and flesh of either fish or meat. Is used as a base for soup or sauces.

FUMET reduced fond.

GLAZE to give dishes a shiny layer by coating with a sweet fluid. Is usually done with cakes, fruit and vegetables and sometimes also with meat.

JULIENNE, À LA to cut into thin strips.

MARINATE/MARINADE meat and vegetables can be given more flavour by letting them soak in a mixture of oil or vinegar combined with herbs or spices.

MONTÉ to thicken a sauce by added pieces of cold butter or egg white. Also gives the sauce a nice sheen.

NAPPÉ to coat a dish with a sauce or gelatine.

PASS THROUGH to pass a dish through a strainer, thus removing seeds and pits.

POACH to cook ingredients in simmering water. Usually done with fish.

QUENCH to add water, stock or wine thus loosening the sediment in a pan.

QUENELLE to form oval shaped balls of fish dough, which can be poached.

REDUCE to reduce the amount of wine or stock by letting it boil.

ROUX mixture of equal parts butter and flour that can be used to thicken sauces.

SAUTÉ to fry in butter, oil or lard on a medium flame.

SEAR to fry vegetables, meat or onions on a medium flame in butter, oil or lard on all sides. The longer you sear the more distinct the taste will be.

SEASONING giving a dish taste, colour or smell by adding herbs or spices

SIMMER to cook in water that is barely boiling.

STEEP to soak dried vegetables and mushrooms in warm water, without letting the water come to a boil.

STEW to cook meat or vegetables that have been seared on a low flame with a lid on the pan.

STIR FRY to cook ingredients in a wok over a high flame with a bit of oil, whilst stirring constantly.

SWEAT to fry on a low flame with hardly any butter, oil or lard in a pan with a thick bottom. Make sure the ingredients don't turn brown.

THICKEN to thicken a sauce by adding flour, butter egg yolks or cream.

ZEST very thin slice of citrus peel.

addresses

alphabetical index

Visit our website and check out Mo' Media's latest publications.

WWW.MOMEDIA.NL

THE RIGHT GUIDE IS PUBLISHED BY MO' MEDIA B.V., P.O. BOX 7028, 4800 GA, BREDA, THE NETHERLANDS,
E-MAIL INFO@MOMEDIA.NL

AUTHOR	harry h harrold
EDITOR	henriëtte straub
TRANSLATING EDITOR	bas straub
PHOTOGRAPHY	maaike koning & patrick wissink (interiors & portraits), joost govers & verne@studio33 (food)
FOOD STYLING	christer elfving & carlo didden
GRAPHIC DESIGN	oranje vormgevers
LITHOGRAPHY	master colors
PRINTING OFFICE	pabo prestige
MANY THANKS TO	maaike van den berg

ISBN 90-5767-050-x

©mo' media, breda, the netherlands, januari 2001

FOR THE SAKE OF GOOD ORDER WE MUST MENTION THAT NONE OF THE RESTAURANTS HAVE PAID TO BE INCLUDED IN THIS GUIDE, NEITHER FOR THE TEXTS, NOR FOR THE PHOTOGRAPHS.